"Marshall King has shone a light on [barcode] is moving story of a young American [barcode] te to peace in a deeply troubled coun [barcode] at is all too rare in this world."
—**ADAM HOCHSCHILD**, author of *King Leopold's Ghost: A Story of Greed, Terror, and Heroism in Colonial Africa*

"Inspiring! Just as sixteenth-century Dirk Willems turned back to rescue his pursuer from drowning, knowing full well the potential consequences, so the story told in this book details a personal pilgrimage in peacebuilding that illuminates the humanity obscured by conflict. Get an inside view of violence and suffering that attends to the unconditional value of a person and posts the waymarkers for healing and building a more peaceful world."
—**MIKE SHERRILL**, CEO of Mennonite Mission Network

"Too often, our heroes are misidentified according to wealth and power. *Disarmed* offers a clear alternative. Within its pages, author Marshall King meticulously details the mysteries surrounding Michael 'MJ' Sharp's murder while illuminating the contours of his ordinary life. There, in that curious contrast, a modern-day hero emerges, the kind who 'leaves seeds.' *Disarmed* is a pasture of wildflowers in wait. I can't wait to put this book in the hands of many, including my own teenagers."
—**SHANNAN MARTIN**, author of *The Ministry of Ordinary Places* and *Falling Free*

"Michael Sharp came to the Democratic Republic of the Congo with an invitation letter signed by me. The Democratic Republic of the Congo has suffered far too long under the world's watch—a world that has enjoyed the country's natural resources. This book tells a story of a courageous and inspirational young man who did not want to be counted among good people who do nothing over this horror and who boldly worked to contribute to peace and recovery of the Congo, working with both local and international actors. This is a moving and inspirational story. Tolle lege!"
—**REV. DR. AMBASSADOR MILENGE MWENELWATA**, national vice president of the Church of Christ in Congo (ECC) and main representative of Kataliko Actions for Africa (KAF) at the United Nations Office at Geneva, Vienna, and New York

"We can't bring peace on earth using human weapons of war. MJ Sharp knew this deep in his bones. Be disarmed as MJ's story breathes new life into how sacrificial love is still the most powerful weapon on the planet to disarm and challenge the violence we see around us today."
—**DIANA K. OESTREICH**, combat soldier turned peacemaker, founder of the Waging Peace Project, and author of *Waging Peace: One Soldier's Story of Putting Love First*

"In our fractured, divisive, and power-hungry world, dare we dream that there are still authentic heroes, pioneers, and martyrs advancing peace against all odds? Can one young, brilliant and compassionate peacemaker from an infinitesimally small countercultural Christian denomination (the Mennonites) really make a bold and beautiful difference on the world stage? Marshall King's *Disarmed* gives us ample proof—in the form of compelling stories and revealing interviews—that the answer, from state departments to on-the-ground guides, is a resounding and brave yes."

—SUSAN SCHULTZ HUXMAN, PhD, president of Eastern Mennonite University

"All of us are born with a peacebuilding superpower. We use it too rarely. MJ Sharp understood the transformative power of listening deeply to, seeing the humanity in, and showing respect for those with a radically different worldview from his own. At a time of deep cultural and political divisions and mistrust, *Disarmed* is the gripping story of how using this superpower allowed MJ to engage others in astonishing and mutually life-changing ways."

—J. DARYL BYLER, advisory board member for the Jimmy and Rosalynn Carter School for Peace and Conflict Resolution at George Mason University and former executive director of the Center for Justice and Peacebuilding at Eastern Mennonite University

"In an era when those who dedicate their lives to championing social justice and peace around the world are ridiculed as 'warriors,' even by those meant to be leading the free world and safeguarding democracy, MJ Sharp's story should be shouted from the rooftops. In the passionate and capable hands of veteran journalist Marshall King, Sharp's life and legacy are reanimated through a story readers will surely never forget even as it inspires them toward deep introspection and self-evaluation."

—CATHLEEN FALSANI, religion journalist and author of *The God Factor* and *Sin Boldly*

"In this book, we have a gift. A gift both for those of us who knew MJ in the flesh and for future generations who will know of this legendary man through the stories we tell. After reading this text, so beautifully situated in the contexts that formed MJ to be who he was, may we all recommit to living fully engaged lives for peace, justice, and joy-filled pranking of violent systems."

—SARAH NAHAR (NEÉ THOMPSON), MJ's friend from high school and professional colleague

DISARMED

*The **Radical Life** and **Legacy** of
Michael "MJ" Sharp*

Marshall V. King

HERALD
P R E S S

Harrisonburg, Virginia

Herald Press
PO Box 866, Harrisonburg, Virginia 22803
www.HeraldPress.com

Library of Congress Cataloging-in-Publication Data
Names: King, Marshall V., 1970- author.
Title: Disarmed : the radical life and legacy of Michael "MJ" Sharp /
    Marshall V. King.
Description: Harrisonburg, Virginia : Herald Press, 2022. | Includes
    bibliographical references.
Identifiers: LCCN 2021047485 (print) | LCCN 2021047486 (ebook) |
    ISBN 9781513808338 (paperback) | ISBN 9781513808345 (hardcover)
    | ISBN 9781513808352 (epub)
Subjects: LCSH: Sharp, MJ (Michael J.), 1982-2017 Mennonites—
    Biography. | Peace—Religious aspects—Christianity. | Nonviolence—
    Religious aspects—Christianity. | BISAC: BIOGRAPHY &
    AUTOBIOGRAPHY / Social Activists | RELIGION / Christian Living /
    Social Issues
Classification: LCC BX8143.S433 K56 2022 (print) | LCC BX8143.S433
    (ebook) | DDC 289.7092—dc23
LC record available at https://lccn.loc.gov/2021047485
LC ebook record available at https://lccn.loc.gov/2021047486

Study guides are available for many Herald Press titles at www.HeraldPress.com.

For the children of MJ's sisters
and best friends: Molly, Jacob, Oscar, Lucy,
Jesse, Brielle, Leo, Jovie, Haven, and Milo.

Contents

Foreword

WHEN NEWS OF the disappearance of Michael "MJ" Sharp and Zaida Catalán reached me, a long exhale ensued. The wisp carried a few unspoken words: *There but for grace . . .*

Disarmed leads us through a biography, a wondrous kaleidoscope of stories of MJ Sharp and his extraordinary sense of purpose. The chapters open age-old truths: Life is a gift. Life is fragile. And in MJ's case, a life cut short has left our world bereft of an exemplar leader.

I recall the early email exchanges with MJ's parents, John and Michele Sharp. We probed and exchanged ideas about a contact or two who might help during the search for MJ and Zaida. I remember the Sharps' warm embrace at the memorial service. Our family paths, MJ's and my own, though separated by a generation, crisscrossed in more than one location—from central Kansas to the valley in Virginia, from Europe to war-torn countries in Africa.

MJ and I never sat together in a classroom. We never directly collaborated on a peacebuilding initiative. But reading through author Marshall King's well-crafted chronicle, I had the clear sense that we shared a common thread of vocation, this inkling of a voice that peace requires more than words. Do justice. Love mercy. Walk humbly. The pursuit of peace takes some walking, not away from but into the fires, full-face toward those myriad challenges that diminish the sacredness of our humanity. It is a vulnerable pathway where the voice calls.

The poet Mark Nepo reflects on the word *vulnerable* by way of its Latin root: *vulnus*—wound. He says the work of vulnerability rises as we learn to carry our wounds gracefully. That sense of grace I certainly experienced with John and Michele.

Threads. In the chapters and voices of friends, family, and professional colleagues, I kept hearing the words of another poet, William Stafford. A Quaker colleague who likely connected with Mennonites as a fellow conscientious objector, Stafford would write in the early morning dark before the physical labor began at the work camps in the 1940s. Near the end of his life, he wrote a poem titled "The Way It Is." His reflections attend to a thread that seeks to be guided by this sense of purpose, the inner voice that calls. While people around us may not understand or even perceive the thread, we stay close, persevere. MJ seemed to hold fast to his thread—a commitment to truth and peace—while staying close to his humor, humility, and humanity, which in turn permitted him to see and touch the humanity of others, even those who wished him harm.

Throughout *Disarmed*, the stories seem to weave back and forth with unspoken questions that people carry but don't quite know how to surface. About purpose and choices. About truth and restoration. I currently serve on an advisory group to the Colombian Truth Commission, led by longtime friend Father Francisco "Pacho" de Roux, who has also spent a lifetime pursuing the thread of peace. He often notes that more than 80 percent of the people killed in the armed violence in his country, which is much like Congo, were his fellow unarmed citizens. Pacho captures the challenge of those unspoken questions in the title of his recent book, *La audacia de la paz imperfecta* (The audacity of the imperfect peace).

Ethics are always a curious endeavor. We have such clarity in the retrospective and prospective musings about the rights and wrongs. The thread of peace, however, requires response in the quality of our presence, in the unfolding moment the gospel of John references as pitching the tent and living among. Ultimately, ethics are revealed in the moment when word becomes flesh.

The heart of the matter seems to be whether we have walked the pathway of woundedness with an open spirit, with eyes that keep noticing that of God in another, and with a tenacious love for that place where truth and grace abound.

This was the audacious pathway MJ chose. His life embodied that spirit.

May his courage and grace inspire us to walk into that tenacious love.

—John Paul Lederach
Professor Emeritus, University of Notre Dame

Author's Note

THIS BOOK IS BUILT on the willingness of more than one hundred people who knew Michael "MJ" Sharp to be interviewed.

In coffee shops and over Zoom, in courtyards in Germany and Albuquerque, and at the kitchen tables of parents who lost their children, I was able to listen and learn about MJ and Zaida Catalán, who both died on March 12, 2017.

It started with MJ's father John, a historian and writer who was an immense help in tracking down details and potential people to interview. MJ's mother Michele, sisters Erin Sharp and Laura Enzinna Sharp, and best friends Andy Gingerich and Keith Grubaugh were all remarkably helpful with this project.

I was able to spend a day in Sweden with Zaida's mother Maria Moresby and sister Elizabeth Moresby, who braided together grace and honesty. In Germany, I spent most of a week at Hausgemeinschaft talking to those who knew and loved MJ. I traveled across the United States, talking to people in person. Others were interviewed by Skype or Zoom.

Videos of MJ's memorial service and numerous stories told that weekend were important resources.

I wasn't able to travel to the Democratic Republic of the Congo, but was able to interview a number of people there via Zoom, WhatsApp, or email.

Most of the quotes in this book, unless otherwise noted, came from all these interviews.

Not everyone whom I contacted to be interviewed was willing to reopen that chapter of their lives, in some cases because it was painful for them to do so.

I never felt that I would be the one to unravel this international murder mystery, and I did not attempt it in this book. Journalists Sonia Rolley and others are far more likely and better poised to do so. The award-winning *Deceptive Diplomacy* was an immense resource for telling that aspect of MJ and Zaida's story.

Staffan Lindberg's book *Mordet på Zaida Catalán*, focused on Zaida and her death, was also a great resource. Though some of Lindberg's reporting and writing is in English, the book is entirely in Swedish, and after consulting a translated version, I confirmed my reading with him.

Using methods I learned as a journalist over the past thirty years, I compiled research starting with the interviews and then going deeper. I used publicly available information, including the Eastern Mennonite University student newspaper, the *Weather Vane*.

I also had access to some of the contents of MJ's computer hard drive after the FBI had spent months cracking MJ's encryption. Many of the documents about the United Nations and Mennonite Central Committee were likely never intended for public scrutiny but were helpful to construct the story of MJ and both his life and work. Jason Garber was able to decrypt some of the files MJ had protected.

Writing a book about someone's life involves far more than just that person's life. I've tried to balance others' privacy and minimize harm, a basic tenet of journalism, as I tell MJ's story in these pages.

—Marshall V. King
September 2021

MJ Sharp holds up a large smallmouth bass he caught on a trip with friends in the Boundary Waters Canoe Area Wilderness in 2001, right after high school graduation. PHOTO COURTESY KEITH GRUBAUGH

There is no way to peace along the way of safety. For peace must be dared, it is itself the great venture and can never be safe. Peace is the opposite of security. To demand guarantees is to want to protect oneself. Peace means giving oneself completely to God's commandment, wanting no security, but in faith and obedience laying the destiny of the nations in the hand of Almighty God, not trying to direct it for selfish purposes. Battles are won, not with weapons, but with God. They are won where the way leads to the cross.

—**DIETRICH BONHOEFFER**, "Peace Speech," as quoted in *Bonhoeffer: Pastor, Martyr, Prophet, Spy*

ONE

A Sunday Walk

MICHAEL J. SHARP knows he is in trouble as he walks barefoot through the Congolese jungle, guided by men carrying guns.

Is his life flashing before his eyes?

We know now what happened, but we will never know what he is thinking in these moments before the end comes.

On this day—March 12, 2017—he is speaking French to the men, probing them and what they are telling him and Zaida Catalán, his coworker with the United Nations.

She walks quietly at the front of the group. The Congolese men answer him in French, though it swirls together with three other languages as they speak to each other. They are armed and wearing red headbands as if they are members of the Kamuina Nsapu, an armed militia group the two UN investigators plan to visit on this day.

MJ, as he was known to many, is unarmed. He isn't even wearing shoes or the Garmin watch with GPS he would usually sport. Their bags, including Zaida's trademark red backpack, aren't slung over their shoulders either. They don't have the cell phones they were carrying when they left Kananga, the largest city nearby where they have been staying.

MJ and Zaida work together on a United Nations Group of Experts, a team of six people who are investigating crimes and human rights abuses in the Democratic Republic of the Congo and reporting to the UN Security Council. On this Sunday, MJ and Zaida are going to meet with the leaders of the Kamuina Nsapu, which has been battling the Armed Forces of the Democratic Republic of the Congo since August 2016 in remote areas in the center of the DRC.

Some of the men in the group walking with MJ and Zaida have cell phones. One takes a call. Another has his hidden at eye-level, recording the interactions as they walk slowly together. MJ and Zaida don't seem to know they're being recorded. While MJ and the men are conversing in French, the rebels are also using Tshiluba, a language common to the Kamuina Nsapu. Swahili and Lingala also mix into the speech, particularly that of the man behind the camera. Lingala is the language of the Congolese army and is considered by members of the Kamuina Nsapu to be impure, the language of *tunguluba*, or "small pigs."

When MJ asks the men what they just said to each other, he's told they're going to the headquarters for the group, that they're waiting for the great chief. MJ senses that the two are not the same thing.

MJ asks if the chief is coming. "Il va venir?"

He's assured that the man will be arriving. A rebel tells him that after they've talked, they'll go to the headquarters, which had been the initial plan.

"But that's akin to lying," MJ tells them. He's probing, the way he would with the picks and rakes in the lockpicking set he'd learned how to use in high school.

One man asks why they would be lying and another assures MJ in broken French that there is no lying happening.

Perhaps it is a bluff. MJ had encountered those in poker games. He had done the bluffing himself in countless games on German military bases, in the living rooms of friends, and at casinos. He won more than he lost at the poker table and used the cash to help fund his education and travels, the purchase of at least one motorcycle, and expenses not covered by meager salaries while working for Mennonite church agencies.

But this is an investigation, not a poker game. MJ's weapons are his intellect and charm. Friends had watched him navigate himself out of speeding tickets, out of nearly being arrested, and to buy time from professors for late papers. "He really could weasel his way out of any situation," said Sgt. Robert Evers, a friend from Germany.

As MJ and Zaida walk with the men, MJ asks them, "Did I come here to attack you?"

"No," says the man holding the video camera.

Perhaps at this moment, MJ's and Zaida's minds are racing. Perhaps they are flipping through the scenes of their lives at speeds they've never seen.

They had come to this place to help the people of the DRC, the way they had other places. Both of them had been to the Middle East on peacemaking trips. Both have been cautious as they do their work in the DRC. They knew that working in a war-torn country is riskier than staying home.

Ten years earlier, MJ's then girlfriend Hannah van Bebber had asked him about his need to do dangerous work. "He said in an ironic way: 'Was soll ich machen, ich wäre halt gerne ein Held und würde gerne die Welt retten.' That translates to 'What should I do? I would love to be a hero and save the world,'" she remembered. It became a joke that they often used with each other as they bantered.

On this Sunday afternoon, finding himself again in the midst of danger, MJ talks calmly to the armed men around him. He is assessing the danger and tells the men with guns and red headbands that the situation is difficult because of the weapons and knives. He is an expert on armed groups, on guns, and he tells them that seeing everyone carrying one is disconcerting.

One man tells another in Tshiluba to speak gently to MJ and Zaida so they remain calm and don't run away.

The men reassure MJ and instruct him and Zaida, who has been walking silently for a bit, to sit down. The pair settle onto the red clay path amid the trees and vegetation.

Zaida tells the men she is a mother. "Moi, j'ai des enfants," she says, though she's never borne a child.

The men talk to each other, and one of them distracts the two UN workers. He rises and steps away from them.

A shotgun fires. MJ crumples to the ground.

₪ ₪ ₪ ₪

Over the years, MJ told his family that his work overseas had risks, but that he had no death wish. His concern was for how they would feel "if something happened to me," he told them. He assured them that he was relatively safe because there would be too many ramifications for someone who tried to kill a white expatriate working for the UN. Since 2000, when the UN had first set up panels or groups in the DRC to serve as eyes and ears for the UN Security Council, not one investigator had been killed.

MJ had been appointed to the group on March 12, 2015, exactly two years before the Sunday afternoon trip to visit the Kamuina Nsapu.

MJ's work in the DRC started in fall 2012. He'd become fluent in French during his time working for Mennonite Central Committee, an agency that does relief work around the world. He was good at learning languages. As a high school senior, he went to Costa Rica for a semester and improved his classroom Spanish. In college, he studied German and then lived, worked, and studied in Germany for five years, first working with soldiers who wanted to quit military service and then going to graduate school to study peacemaking. When he took the job in eastern Congo with Mennonite Central Committee, he went to Brussels to start learning French and then honed the language as he worked in the DRC. One of his roles was urging leaders of one of the country's armed militia groups to allow child soldiers to leave the forest and go home.

He had fallen in love with this country that he called paradise. Few in the world even think of the DRC as they look down at their cell phones containing bits of coltan extracted from the country's soil. Nor do they know how the mining of copper and cobalt, as well as gold and diamonds, continues to fuel corruption and violence in this African nation.

The DRC is one of the world's richest countries in terms of natural resources but one of the poorest in terms of per capita income. It's the place about which Joseph Conrad wrote *Heart of Darkness*, a lightly fictionalized account of the violence and atrocity he witnessed there in the late 1800s.

At that time, King Leopold II of Belgium was exploiting the land and its people, extracting ivory and rubber from the country then just called Congo. He treated the country as his corporation, run on the backs of enslaved people who lost hands, limbs, or their lives as they struggled to meet quotas enacted by the Belgians. After Belgium left Congo in 1960, unrest continued under a series of corrupt leaders.

The powerful Congo River could provide enough electricity for the entire continent. The rich mines could provide income and infrastructure for the entire country. Instead, the country remains one of the world's poorest and most dangerous places to live.

ᴎ ᴎ ᴎ ᴎ

Much of the country's violence is in eastern Congo, where many of the hundred or so armed militia groups are based and where MJ first worked. He lived in Bukavu, a city near Lake Kivu, one of a series called the Great Lakes. Far from the Great Lakes of the United States near which MJ had grown up, Lake Kivu borders Rwanda, where revenge and violence still arise from the wounds and scars of the 1994 genocide.

War and violence are part of daily life for many of the approximately ninety million people in the DRC, particularly in eastern Congo. In his role with MCC, MJ helped some of the 1.4 million internally displaced persons in that part of the country. He became an expert on the rebel group Forces démocratiques pour la libération, most often called FDLR.

He was less familiar with the Kasai-Central province, a chunk of land in the center of the country about the size of the US state of Georgia. In 2016, violence had flared in this province between the group known as Kamuina Nsapu and the Congolese army Forces armées de la république démocratique du Congo (FARDC). More than four hundred people were killed and more than two hundred thousand were displaced by the ensuing violence, according to the UN. The Kamuina Nsapu were using child soldiers carrying wooden guns with the belief that witchcraft would make the guns work and protect them from enemy bullets. The FARDC was believed to be burying dead civilians in mass graves near the town of Tshimbulu. When soldiers from United Nations Organization Stabilization Mission in the DR Congo, better known by its French acronym MONUSCO, tried to investigate the mass graves, soldiers in the Congolese FARDC army confronted the UN soldiers and tried to keep them from visiting possible sites.

ᴎ ᴎ ᴎ ᴎ

MJ grew up in a Mennonite home absent of guns until he got a BB gun and a long safety lesson from his grandfather Mahlon. That BB gun remained unloaded except for the times when MJ asked for permission to remove it from the safe location and use it.

The first time he went deer hunting with Grandpa, they prepared diligently in a room above the garage. On the morning of the hunt, Grandma Dorothy fixed them a big breakfast, and they spent hours sitting quietly in the deer stand.

MJ didn't enjoy that first hunt. He tried to come up with how to gently tell his grandfather he didn't like hunting as much as he thought he would.

When they got in the truck, Grandpa said excitedly, "Isn't God's creation wonderful?"

MJ kept quiet. And he kept going along to hunt until he also became hooked.

From those precious times with his grandfather, he knew how to fire a gun and how to shoot an animal. But he chose other weapons as a pacifist working in the world to bring peace.

Both MJ's father John and his grandfather were Mennonite pastors. They were among those who taught MJ that conscientious objectors don't go to war, they don't bear arms, and they don't join the military. They understood Jesus' Sermon on the Mount in the New Testament book of Matthew as the guide for living, a companion piece to the Ten Commandments in the Old Testament.

Yet MJ also understood that refusing to fight was different from refusing to engage those who did. He became a living paradox as one of the few Mennonites who could be called an expert on guns and US military armaments as he worked with soldiers who wanted to become conscientious objectors. In Germany, he worked with the Military Counseling Network from 2005 to 2008, learning how to speak the language of a soldier and employing it to conduct conversations about peace. In the DRC, he walked into the camps of rebel groups unarmed and would sit for hours, listening and talking to commanders in an effort to get them to allow soldiers to be able to leave the forest and return home.

Zaida Catalán was a Swedish expert on human rights abuses and was also a pacifist; however, she felt differently about guns than MJ. When she worked for the European Union Police Mission in Afghanistan, she was urged to receive training on how to handle a gun. She wanted no part of it. "She didn't want to learn how to shoot, how to hold a gun," her mother Maria Moresby said.

Their job as investigators on the Group of Experts was to study the violence in the DRC and report to the UN Security Council on its sources. MJ focused on armed groups. Zaida focused on human rights. They had to immerse themselves in this place and catalog the ways violence was being done by humans to other humans.

It was heartbreaking work.

"I think it was the mission of her life to help other people," said Maria as she sat in a coffee shop in Kalmar, a small city on the southeastern coast of Sweden.

Zaida had been a rising political star in Sweden. She had run for Parliament as a young member of the Green Party before abandoning politics for a different form of bringing change and justice into the world. That work started to take her to some of the world's hot spots. She'd been to Jerusalem and Palestine. She'd survived a suicide bombing.

In 2012, she had gone to work in Goma, DRC, teaching women and police about fighting gender-based violence in a country where rape is as common a weapon as guns and machetes. She joined the Group of Experts in 2016 to continue that work.

"It wasn't their country. They did it for others," said Maria. "They were extraordinarily normal, but loving, compassionate people."

〣 〣 〣 〣

On March 11, 2017—the day before the trip into the jungle— MJ and Zaida sit in a room at Wood Land Guest House, where they are staying, and ask a representative of the Kamuina Nsapu whether they will be safe making this passage on a Sunday to visit the group.

MJ makes it clear to the six men seated around the glass-topped table that he and Zaida are investigators for the United Nations and have come to speak to locals about the violence that has emerged over the recent months. Zaida secretly records the meeting, and sunlight streams in the open doors to the outside.

MJ asks several times if they will be safe and they receive assurances from some of the men.

Michael "MJ" Sharp and Zaida Catalán meet with interpreters and tribal leaders on March 11, 2017, in this photo from Zaida's phone. PHOTO USED BY PERMISSION OF MORESBY FAMILY

The elderly man listens to the question translated into the local language Tshiluba and urges them not to go. "You do not know what happens there. … They will be attacked," he says to the translator.

The translator, in French, assures MJ and Zaida that they will be fine to make the trip to Bunkonde.

MJ and Zaida have no way of understanding the lie.

The next morning, MJ texts his friend Sonia Rolley, "We'll be down south today to meet some of the groups. Should be back before too late to catch up." The veteran French journalist is traveling with a Reuters journalist in the same area where Zaida and MJ are planning to go.

As is their practice when they aren't traveling together in the Congo, MJ contacts Christoph Vogel, one of the four other members of the Group of Experts. As the two specialists on armed groups, MJ and Christoph have conducted nearly every investigation together except this one that MJ and Zaida are doing. The two men had become close friends and usually call each other, morning and night, to update each other on their joint work. Because of Christoph's poor cell phone coverage, they exchange only texts on this morning, wishing each other a safe trip.

At breakfast around nine, MJ and Zaida indicate to an acquaintance that their trip has been delayed because of an issue with securing the motorcycles and that they aren't happy. They leave the guesthouse around nine thirty on the backs of two motorcycles driven by Congolese men and accompanied by a translator.

They travel that morning, encountering checkpoints and others working in the area. In the middle of the day, a representative from Caritas International, a Catholic relief agency, sees them on the backs of the motorcycles.

At 3:49 p.m. central European time, Elizabeth Moresby's phone rings as she is preparing dinner with Maria Moresby at the family home in Öland, off the eastern coast of Sweden. It appears Zaida is calling her younger sister from the DRC.

Elizabeth answers the call. She and Maria hear men's voices on speakerphone. Together they listen to the voices for seventy-two seconds.

Then Elizabeth can hear breathing. She believes it is Zaida. The call ends.

ᴎ ᴎ ᴎ ᴎ

After Elizabeth gets the call, she alerts the United Nations in New York City. A few hours later she's informed that a security protocol has been enacted and a search is on for the experts.

Christoph and others also realize something isn't right. When he doesn't get a text from MJ indicating they are back from visiting the Kamuina Nsapu, he tries to call both MJ and Zaida. About ten that night, someone answers Zaida's phone. "I had the same sensation Zaida's family had," Christoph said. "I heard some remote voices mumbling and couldn't establish contact with anyone on the phone who had picked up."

That call worries him. He begins to imagine what could have happened to his colleagues. "I became much more worried. Why would someone pick up a phone and then not talk?" he said.

That was the beginning of two difficult weeks for the families of MJ and Zaida and others who knew the two.

Within hours, the United Nations had confirmed that the pair and those with them were missing, believed to have been kidnapped. Michael's parents John and Michele Sharp, after learning the news, shared it with his sisters, Erin and Laura.

That Monday, Michele called Erin on her thirty-seventh birthday and wished her a happy birthday. Then she told her that her brother was missing. "I immediately started crying and said this can't be happening. This can't be happening," Erin said.

Michele called MJ's younger sister Laura and told her to hand her three-week-old infant to her mother-in-law and sit down. Then she broke the news. "I didn't have an emotional response though," said Laura. "I just wanted to know what details we knew, and what was being done to find him."

In the DRC, Christoph and others began calling their contacts seeking information. Soldiers from MONUSCO searched for the missing investigators. The other trained investigators in the UN team worked every channel to get information. Other researchers and journalists, including Sonia Rolley, did the same thing.

The rumors flip-flopped. A drafted press release on Monday, March 13, from the DRC government indicated they'd been killed. The release was never sent, and instead the public communication was that they were missing.

The US Federal Bureau of Investigations started working the case because it involved a kidnapping of a US citizen. The initial news stories indicated that six people had been kidnapped. In addition to MJ and Zaida, the three motorcycle drivers and an interpreter were believed to be missing.

For those searching for answers, a good day had more indications that they were alive. A bad one had more indications they were dead. As days passed, there were more bad days than good days.

Friends in the Congo and around the world offered prayers for MJ and Zaida and for their families. This young man who was missing had lived in most of the larger Mennonite communities in the United States in Pennsylvania, Indiana, and Virginia. He had ties to people in all of them and also in central Kansas, where his parents lived. On March 15, a simultaneous prayer vigil gathered Mennonites at locations across the United States. In Indiana, Kansas, New Mexico, and Colorado, folks gathered and prayed, "God, bearer of peace and warrior of justice, may your presence surround your child, MJ, and may our prayers shine light upon his face and bring comfort to his soul. May your Holy Spirit commune with his spirit and usher him to your safe arms of rest and peace. May your presence bring solace and strength to the three drivers, translator, and Zaida [Catalán]."

News stories broke in local, national, and international outlets in the United States, Europe, and Africa. The stories delineated how MJ approached rebels in the Congo and listened to them, how he forged relationships with people who were unlike him. John and Michele Sharp fielded interview requests and spoke of their son and his work to bring peace to places and people who struggled to find it.

Those who knew him repeatedly assured themselves and each other by saying, "If there's anyone who can talk their way out of any situation, it's Michael."

His parents were getting updates from UN officials, FBI agents, and those who knew MJ in the DRC and were trying to find out what happened. The family members agreed to their phones being tapped in case a kidnapper called.

Such a call never came.

The search ended on March 26. Fourteen days after they went missing, the bodies of Michael and Zaida were discovered in a shallow grave and recovered by MONUSCO. The identities were confirmed on March 27, Michele's birthday.

Zaida's mother Maria and sister Elizabeth got a knock on the door in the middle of the night telling them about the discovery. John and Michele, who had been fielding calls and staying in touch with family and friends from their Hesston home, knew two FBI agents were coming that Monday morning to share news with them.

The dreaded knock on the door that so many military families know may come when a family member is potentially in harm's way isn't common for Mennonites. It's a rare thing for a federal official to relay news of an international death. Yet here were John and Michele, with their daughters Erin and Laura and Erin's husband Alex and Laura's husband Nick, hearing that the body of their son and his colleague had been found in a shallow grave. They had gathered at John and Michele's home in Kansas hoping to hear news that he had been found alive. Instead they learned he had been killed while trying to bring peace to a violent place.

They had been preparing for this day long before March 12.

"I gave MJ and his work to God. On a daily basis," said Michele. "I have been working ever since he started his work at giving him up."

She knew that someday she might lose him. The day had come. She and others who loved MJ weren't truly ready. Their beloved son had died doing this peacebuilding work on the other side of the world.

₪ ₪ ₪ ₪

John and others in the family have often said that MJ died as he lived: "fully engaged."

He was engaging those around him, probing with questions, when one of the men wearing a red headband fired a shot that killed him instantly. The single shotgun blast occured a few seconds after Zaida frantically told the more than a dozen men around them that she was a mother.

She screamed and tried to scramble away. One of the men shot and killed her.

MJ's and Zaida's blood seeped into the soil of a country whose people and land they loved.

After the men killed Zaida, they cut off her head. Others in this conflict between the government forces and Kamuina Nsapu are not just killed, but beheaded. It's indignity added to death.

When the bodies are discovered two weeks later, the tattoo on Zaida's left wrist, "Per aspera ad astra" (Latin for "Through adversity to the stars"), helps identify her.

₪ ₪ ₪ ₪

The Sharps traveled to John F. Kennedy International Airport to meet their son's body, then they sat with his body in a wooden casket in a Delaware funeral home. They met with FBI, State Department, and UN officials in New York City to hear updates on the investigation of their son's death. Little was known about the deaths other than that they were shot and Zaida was beheaded.

As the families grieved, tribute after tribute appeared on Facebook and in email inboxes. A torrent of stories, laments, and photos from friends and family poured forth.

At a funeral on April 15 in Hesston, Kansas, where MJ's parents now live, hundreds gathered to remember MJ's amazing life, full of passion, compassion, and wit. David Stutzman, MJ's former colleague in Germany, said, "To me, losing Michael feels like losing a brother in arms. I like to use the military metaphor. I think that's something Michael would have liked."

In the days after the funeral, after most friends had returned home, the investigation into the deaths continued. On social media, in interviews, and via letters, John Sharp called for the UN not to stop its peacekeeping efforts, and he called on President Donald Trump not to cut funding for the UN. John and Michele also asked this of UN officials, including Secretary-General António Guterres and US Ambassador to the United Nations Nikki Haley.

The families hoped for the truth to emerge. They weren't expecting that would come through a video that would traumatize them further.

The first time the video was shown, at least publicly, was by the government of the DRC. On April 24, 2017, just days after the memorial services for MJ, the DRC government called a press conference and showed journalists the video. Government officials claimed they had found the video, which had been taken on a hidden cell phone, and that it proved Kamuina Nsapu was responsible for the deaths. The men whom the video shows carrying out these acts of violence were wearing that group's signature red headbands.

Over six minutes and seventeen grueling seconds, the video shows the full horror of what happened that day in the jungle: the conversations, the shootings, and worse.

Many who watched the video through the lens of their work with the UN or advocacy organizations in the DRC didn't believe the government's claims. In the coming months, analysis of the video and other claims by government officials led many to believe that the Congolese government, at least at some level, was involved in the deaths and that the Kamuina Nsapu had not acted on its own.

The Moresbys watched the full video. Maria said she wanted to know what happened to her daughter. Most of MJ's family members and close friends watched only the portion before the shooting, and MJ's sister Laura watched the entire thing.

ꗢ ꗢ ꗢ ꗢ

In her final posting to Twitter nine days before her death, Zaida had retweeted a line attributed to Buddha: "Three things cannot be long hidden: the sun, the moon, and the truth."

The video became a weapon in the war on truth. Though it revealed some of what happened on March 12, 2017, it didn't lead to immediate action by the DRC government to find the men in the video. The government reported arrests along the way, but for several years the investigations have moved slowly and often in puzzling directions.

As the truth of their deaths remains clouded, others around the world continue to tell stories of MJ and Zaida, of their impact on the world.

John and Michele Sharp tell other Mennonites about their son and how he helped broker peace, helped people find ways other than violence. They tell of how he lived thirty-four years fully engaged.

The friends, the former girlfriends, the coworkers tell stories of how MJ made them laugh, of how he was their hero. They debate whether he would have wanted to be famous.

Some days, he just wanted to be the Dude, the mythic character played by Jeff Bridges in the 1998 Coen Brothers movie *The Big Lebowski*, a quirky tale of mistaken identity, bowling, and a guy trying to live his life with his friends.

In speaking about his best friend at the memorial service, Andy Gingerich invoked a line from their favorite movie, saying, "I was his dude. He was my hero. But what's a hero?"

For true evangelical faith is of such a nature that it cannot lay dormant; but manifests itself in all righteousness and works of love; it dies unto flesh and blood; destroys all forbidden lusts and desires; cordially seeks, serves, and fears God; clothes the naked; feeds the hungry; consoles the afflicted; shelters the miserable; aids and consoles all the oppressed; returns good for evil; serves those that injure it; prays for those that persecute it; teaches, admonishes, and reproves with the Word of the Lord; seeks that which is lost; binds up that which is wounded; heals that which is diseased; and saves that which is sound. The persecution, suffering, and anxiety which befalls it for the sake of the truth of the Lord, is to it a glorious joy and consolation.

—**MENNO SIMONS**, *The Reason Why Menno Simon* [sic] *Does Not Cease Teaching and Writing*

TWO

The Mennonite Way

BEHIND A COUNTER at Goshen Brewing Company in Goshen, Indiana, a shirt is for sale with the face of Menno Simons.

His visage is attached to a set of arms, as buff and thick as a weightlifter's. A half-full glass with the brewing company's logo is next to him. And the words below read "Menno-Mighty."

The shirt is an odd and playful mix of disparate elements—like MJ himself. The face of Menno Simons, the man for whom an entire religious group is named, isn't always used with utmost reverence. Some Mennonite churches have handheld fans attached to wooden sticks with his picture on the thin cardboard and the words "I'm a Menno Simons fan."

The playful treatment of Menno Simons belies the difficulty he faced in leading disparate groups rebelling against both the Catholic and Protestant churches and political leaders of the day in Europe in the 1500s. It's clear from his humble writings that he would never have envisioned being seen as the father of a group called Mennonites that now numbers 2.1 million worldwide, with some of the largest groups in the United States, Canada, and the Democratic Republic of the Congo.

In July 1999, MJ's father John used a cartoonish drawing of Menno Simons during a presentation dubbed "Heroes and Anabaptism" at the convention for American and Canadian Mennonites. The line in the program for the thousands attending the biannual gathering in St. Louis read, "So you think Anabaptist history is filled with boring stories to put you to sleep? Wake up and learn about some of the truly exciting and even heroic stories of our ancient ancestors."

Because his father was both a pastor and a historian, MJ grew up hearing about early Anabaptists and Mennonites. He knew the stories of Menno Simons and others who helped shape a faith, a way of viewing the world, based on the premise that nonviolent peacemaking can be used to counter violence. MJ's passion for creatively solving problems using a different form of might drew from the bold faith of his ancestors.

Menno was born in Witmarsum, in the present-day Netherlands, in 1496. The son of a farmer, he spent his early years in school at a monastery, and at the age of fifteen began formal training to become a Catholic priest. By the age of twenty, he was a deacon in the Catholic Church. As a young priest, he didn't read the Bible. He later said he spent much of that time drinking, playing cards, and other diversions. Yet he became the leader of a reform movement that has lasted for generations.

ℼ ℼ ℼ ℼ

On a January night in 1525, a group of about fifteen people gathered at the home of Felix Manz and his mother Anna. A man called George Blaurock asked Conrad Grebel, one of the foremost leaders of this circle of believers, to pour water on him as a "true Christian baptism."[1]

The choice to be baptized as an adult was part of their critique of an intertwined church and state that baptized infants. In the New Testament, Jesus had called disciples to follow him and live in new ways, but to do so voluntarily and inevitably in ways that countered the powerful religious and government leaders of the era. In Europe, Christians had historically baptized infants, assuring that their sins were forgiven and that all society was unified as followers of Christ. These were the first rebaptisms for this group of Reformers, eight years after Martin Luther had declared the need for the whole of the church to be reformed.

Early Anabaptist history is full of bloodshed and even a few calls for violence among leaders who were encouraging followers to take stands on infant baptism. Yet over time, the Anabaptists, or literally "re-baptizers," rejected the state and its violent approach to problem-solving. Jesus' call to "love your enemies, do good to those who hate you" (Luke 6:27) was taken seriously, as was Mark 16:16, which reads, "The one who believes and is baptized will be saved; but the one who does not believe will be condemned."

Anabaptists, then and now, assert that a baby cannot choose to believe and that belief can happen only after a person comes to an age of reckoning, when one can comprehend that one is a sinner and in need of God's forgiveness and grace.

In modern societies, the difference between infant baptism and getting baptized later in life is seen as a difference in religious practice or even a cultural difference, but not one over which people would be willing to die. In the early 1500s, however, it became a cause for which people would give their lives.

In early 1527, two years after the home baptism, Felix Manz became one of the first Anabaptist martyrs and the first to die at the hands of the Protestants. In Zurich, Manz was charged with setting up a separate church from the sanctioned Protestant and Catholic ones and was sentenced to death in a statement that read in part, "Manz shall be delivered to the executioner, who shall tie his hands, put him into a boat, take him to the lower hut, there strip his bound hands down over his knees, place a stick between his knees and arms, and thus push him into the water and let him perish in the water; thereby he shall have atoned to the law and justice."[2]

As he was taken to the boat, Manz praised God. He testified that he was about to die for the truth. His mother and brothers in the crowd encouraged him to stay strong in the faith. As he was being bound, his final words before an executioner drowned him in the icy Limmat River were "In manus tuas, Domine, commendo spiritum meum," or "Into your hands,

MJ overlooks the Limmat River in the early 2000s near where Felix Manz was drowned for his beliefs. PHOTO PROVIDED BY TIM AND HEIDI HUBER, USED WITH PERMISSION

Lord, I commend my spirit." It was the same thing Jesus said as he hung on the cross during his crucifixion.

John Sharp once stood on the shore of that river overlooking the spot where Manz drowned and retold the story to his son. MJ told his father, "Wow, I wonder if I could do that."

Six weeks after Manz's death, Anabaptists gathered in Schleitheim, a northern Switzerland town where the budding movement had taken hold, to clarify the beliefs and practices of this group that had come to be known as Swiss Brethren. Michael Sattler, a former Benedictine who became one of the movement's leaders and was himself later martyred, wrote the statement that was ratified by the gathering on February 24, 1527. What they called "Brotherly Union of a Number of Children of God Concerning Seven Articles" came to be known as the Schleitheim Confession.

The seven convictions or topics, which still undergird aspects of modern Mennonite life, were as follows:

- Adult baptism: Baptism is offered to those who confess their sins and claim the resurrection of Jesus.

- "The ban," or excommunication: Adults who stray from church teachings can be banned from the group of believers.

- Communion: Those who are baptized remember the crucifixion and resurrection of Jesus Christ with breaking of bread and sharing a cup of grape juice or wine.

- Separation: "A separation shall be made from the evil and from the wickedness which the devil planted in the world."[3]

- Pastors: Leaders guide the church of God as shepherds would guide a flock of sheep and keep it safe from harm, sometimes even through discipline.

- The sword: Jesus commanded followers to employ love instead of violence. The confession also stated that government involvement isn't appropriate for Christians who are citizens of heaven instead of the world.

- Taking oaths: Jesus prohibited swearing in God's name for any reason. Promises can be made, but in the form of simply "yea and nay."

The stories of Anabaptist martyrdom infuse sermons and history courses at Mennonite high schools and colleges. MJ and a classmate at Bethany Christian High School in the late 1990s would pore over the stories in *Martyrs Mirror*, a volume of over a thousand pages first published in 1660 delineating the people who had died for their religious beliefs, starting with Jesus followers in the first century and continuing through Anabaptists killed in the several years before publication.

The English translation of this thick book sits on bookshelves in many European-American Mennonite homes. The 104 illustrations that became part of the book in its second edition in 1685 capture the imaginations of youngsters. The book is full of tales of violence done to people who believed so deeply in their way of following Jesus that they refused to recant and died in horrible fashion: Anabaptists who had their tongues cut out, who were burned at the stake and beheaded, who were drowned.

The most famous martyr story is that of Dirk Willems, who in 1569 was imprisoned in southern Holland. According to *Martyrs Mirror*, he escaped from prison and crossed a body of water covered by thin ice. The "thief-catcher" pursuing him fell through. Instead of assuring his own freedom by running on, Willems returned to save the man's life. The thief-catcher advocated for his release, but the burgomaster, or mayor of the town, demanded Willems's return to prison, and he was burned at the stake in May 1569. The engraving of Willems reaching for his pursuer is an image that is embedded in Mennonite imagination and psyche, illustrating how those who follow Jesus are to do good to those who would harm them and to love their enemies, even at the risk of their own personal peril.

In this Anabaptists were at odds with both Catholic and Protestant Christians, who believed that one could fight or participate in the military as long as the cause was holy or just. That stance of nonviolence, rooted in Jesus' commands to love at all costs, became a marker for those who became Mennonite or one of the dozens of other groups to spring from Anabaptist roots.

₪ ₪ ₪ ₪

As the movement grew from the 1600s to the 1800s in Europe and then North America, some Anabaptists became successful farmers or entrepreneurs while others continued to be persecuted. An increasing number started calling themselves Mennonite rather than Anabaptist, which became an umbrella term identifying a growing number of groups. Perhaps the use of the ban to deal with church members who were at odds with the teaching of the church can be blamed for the ways Anabaptists have splintered into what are now around forty different groups of Mennonites, Brethren, and Amish.

The most significant group to arise out of one such division is the Amish, whose distinctive dress and intentional and communal decisions about how to embrace technology and modernity have made the group a source of both fascination and parody in the United States.

In the late 1600s, a preacher named Jakob Ammann urged Mennonites to stay separate from the world and use the discipline of shunning, or excommunication, to maintain church purity. Conversations between Ammann and other Mennonite leaders turned into an angry dispute and separation in 1693. Ammann's followers, who maintained simple dress and practiced footwashing and regular communion, became known as Amish. The Amish continue to champion community and simple living as part of their commitment to maintaining order.

Mennonites and, later, Amish began migrating to the United States about the same time the Amish and Mennonites were splitting. In 1683, a group of thirteen households, including one Mennonite family, sailed from northern Germany to southeastern Pennsylvania and founded a village called Germantown. The burg included Quakers, Mennonites, Lutherans, and Reformed and was the first successful settlement of Mennonites in North America. By 1699, the village had enough Mennonites to form the first Mennonite congregation in North America.

During the first half of the 1700s, Mennonites and Amish were among the waves of European immigrants coming to the United States. Some moved to the Shenandoah Valley of Virginia in the 1730s. Others found their way to Mifflin County, Pennsylvania, by the 1790s, Holmes and Wayne Counties in Ohio by 1810, and farther west to Indiana, Illinois, and Iowa by the 1860s.

Mennonites from Russia, where another branch of the Anabaptist tree had sprouted, also started migrating to North America. The first group of eighteen thousand arrived in the 1870s, settling in Kansas, Oklahoma, and South Dakota, as well as the Canadian province of Manitoba. In many cases, families found their way to farmland near the same latitude as their homelands in Russia and western Europe. Mennonites and other Anabaptists in North America tended to work hard and gain the respect of those around them. Many avoided civic involvement because of their beliefs, though Amish engaged in local politics until about 1850.

א א א א

After an act of violence, Amish and Mennonites often make headlines for their bold acts of extending forgiveness.

After a gunman in Lancaster County, Pennsylvania, shot ten girls in a one-room Amish schoolhouse in 2006, killing five of them, the Amish leaders emphasized forgiveness and reconciliation that shocked many outsiders. People took notice when members of the Amish community attended the shooter's funeral after his suicide and set up a charitable fund for his family, and wanted to know more about this countercultural—and biblical—commitment to forgiveness.

European and North American Mennonites have been labeled "the quiet in the land." MJ's ancestors believed that violence wasn't the answer to problems and only created more. Some faced persecution or even prosecution for refusing military service. And a growing number ventured into the world to do missionary or service work to spread that gospel of peace.

Throughout World War I and World War II, Mennonite young men became conscientious objectors to avoid bearing arms. Between the wars, peace churches worked to create Civilian Public Service, sending young men to work in mental hospitals and to fight wildfires in the western United States. During the Korean War, men (and some women) served in similar alternative roles through 1-W Service.

Writer Norman Maclean, in his book *Young Men and Fire*, quotes a character describing the Mennonites who became smokejumpers in the 1940s:

"Them sons-of-bitches," he said . . . "was Mennonites and wouldn't fight in the last war—said they wasn't afraid to work or die for their country but wouldn't kill anybody, so somebody, maybe for this somebody's idea of a joke, had them sent to the Smokejumpers. It turned out them sons-of-bitches was farm boys and, what's more, didn't believe in using machines no way—working was just for their hands and their horses, and them sons-of-bitches took them shovels and saws and Pulaskis and put a hump in their backs and never straightened up until morning when they had a fire-line around the whole damn fire. Them sons-of-bitches was the world's champion firefighters."[4]

Experiences "in the world" almost certainly led to other changes among American Mennonites. In the twentieth century, Mennonites began to move out of farming communities and to more urban settings and became more racially and ethnically diverse, but the communities in which European and Russian immigrants originally settled in the eighteenth and nineteenth centuries remain hubs for Anabaptist groups.

The experiences doing service "for the least of these" at home or in missionary and relief settings across the world changed the perspectives and practices of those as they returned. Mennonites returning from mental health hospitals during 1-W service were inspired to open their own community mental health centers to provide more humane care.

Some Mennonites became active in social justice causes. Others became teachers, social workers, and nurses. Business owners found success, in some cases by offering hospitality experiences to tourists curious about Amish and Mennonite life and food.

In 1920, the Mennonite Brethren Church, Mennonite Church, and General Conference Mennonite Church had come together to help provide relief for those affected by the Ukrainian famine exacerbated by the Russian Civil War. Two graduates of Goshen College, a Mennonite college in northern Indiana, went to gather information about the crisis in the village of Halbstadt, the German name for the Mennonite settlement in present-day Zaporizhia Oblast, Ukraine. After consulting with leaders there, Orie Miller returned to Constantinople to organize the response to the needs in Halbstadt and the rest of the Molotschna Colony. Even though the Reds were quickly gaining ground, Clayton Kratz believed he would be safe as a relief worker and an American. But when the Red Army over-ran the village, he was arrested by the new local Soviet authority and was never heard from again.

Like the stories in *Martyrs Mirror*, the story of how Clayton Kratz risked his life to help others and likely died doing so is often taught to Mennonite young people in Sunday school and Mennonite high school and college classes. This story would have been particularly familiar to MJ; his father penned a book on Orie Miller, who became the leader of Mennonite Central Committee.

The practice of working on behalf of others, of living for others, weaves its way through Mennonite life. A quote from Menno Simons's writings was turned into a song with these lyrics: "True evangelical faith cannot lie sleeping, / for it clothes the naked, / it comforts the sorrowful, / it gives to the hungry, food, / and it shelters the destitute. / It cares for the blind and lame, / the widow and orphan child. / That's true evangelical faith. / It binds up the wounded man, it offers a gentle hand. It has become everything to all men."[5] At MJ's memorial service, his friend Andy Gingerich performed the song, which he and MJ had learned and sang together at Bethany Christian High School. Andy said it exemplified MJ's life and work.

The life and words of a Radical Reformer who was part of a sixteenth-century movement continue to shape how a small group of followers choose to live out their Christianity. That understanding is part of what propelled Michael Jesse "MJ" Sharp into the world nearly five hundred years later.

It's funny: I always imagined when I was a kid that adults had some kind of inner toolbox, full of shiny tools: the saw of discernment, the hammer of wisdom, the sandpaper of patience. But when I grew up I found that life handed you these rusty bent tools— friendships, prayer, conscience, honesty—and said, Do the best you can with these, they will have to do. And mostly, against all odds, they're enough.

—ANNE LAMOTT, *Traveling Mercies*

THREE

An All-American Boy

MJ SHARP CAME out fighting.

Perhaps that's an odd thing to say about a baby who would grow up to become a Mennonite peacemaker, yet in that Elkhart General Hospital delivery room, MJ needed to fight for his life: his umbilical cord was tightly wrapped twice around his neck, and he came out blue and not ready to breathe. His mother Michele remembers the moment he filled his lungs with air and cried out as if to say, "I'm here, folks! Watch out, world!"

Michele looked over at her worried husband and said, "John, you have a son."

That was October 29, 1982. The young couple had a two-and-a-half-year-old daughter, Erin, who came to the hospital to visit her young brother before he arrived home at the corner of Roys and Garfield Avenues in Elkhart, Indiana. In that small, two-story house with wood siding, across from the playground of an elementary school, they raised a family as they studied at and worked for Mennonite institutions.

John was preparing to be a pastor, studying at Associated Mennonite Biblical Seminaries, now called Anabaptist Mennonite Biblical Seminary. Michele was working for the Mennonite Board of Missions.

As John was learning the Anabaptist story and how early martyrs had died for their faith, Michele turned to her husband and said, "If you had to choose between faith and family, you'd end up choosing faith, wouldn't you?"

He replied, "Wouldn't you want me to?"

Michele said she would and acknowledged that she would probably do the same. Little did they know how their son would someday wrestle with the same question.

ℕ ℕ ℕ ℕ

When the Sharp's third child, Laura, was born in April 1985, young MJ greeted her by saying he wanted to "spit on her," which became one of many family stories that get repeated with laughter. Michele started calling her son a "schnickelfritz," the word for a cute, rambunctious child in the Low German dialect called Pennsylvania Dutch spoken by Amish and some Mennonites, including John, Michele, and many of their ancestors. The three children were all two and a half years apart and played well with each other. When Erin dressed up, MJ wanted to as well. He was higher energy than she was, and she remembers him running circles around her.

That running landed him in the hospital one day when he was three years old. Soon after the birth of Laura, he was running in the hallways of the church where his father was now a pastor and broke his femur. The young boy was in traction for a time and used a wheeled cart to move himself around until he could walk again. He started walking again on the same day his younger sister walked for the first time, though she won that competition by a few hours.

In 1989, John was hired as the pastor of Scottdale Mennonite Church in Scottdale, Pennsylvania. The small town thirty miles southeast of Pittsburgh was home to the Mennonite Publishing House, which produced Sunday school materials, Herald Press books, and other resources used by English-speaking Mennonites. Rust Belt–era iron and steel mills nearby employed many of the people in the area, but it was "the Pub" that attracted educated Mennonites with a creative streak to help tend the printed word for the tribe of English-speaking Mennonites. Many in the congregation had lived or served in other parts of the world. John was the lone pastor of the church and thoroughly enjoyed leading the congregation. Michele found work as a substitute teacher.

Erin and MJ attended the elementary school in town. When he was in the first grade, administrators tested MJ for the gifted program at Alverton Elementary School. He made it in, but a friend didn't. The boy told his mother, "MJ thinks he is smarter than I am because he got into the program."

That was a misunderstanding. Michele remembers MJ being distraught that he got into the program and his friend didn't. Their attempts to smooth things over with the other family didn't go well. A counselor helped them see that MJ was depressed. John had experienced severe depression in the past and acknowledged the family history. The counselor continued to work with them throughout MJ's elementary school experience.

MJ's family saw his brilliance more and more during his early years. When John and Michele were doing multiplication tables with Erin at the kitchen table, MJ started answering before his older sister.

He often demonstrated how quick-witted he was, how nimbly his mind worked. One morning when MJ walked into a bathroom at a relative's house, he encountered a naked soon-to-be aunt who had just gotten out of the shower.

"Don't you knock?" asked an alarmed Debbie.

"Don't you lock?" he returned without a pause.

The Iowa Tests of Basic Skills in 1994, when MJ was in sixth grade, placed him in the ninetieth percentile in every category, including ninety-eighth in work study skills and ninety-ninth in science. Those responsible for educating him, in creating an individualized education program, noted that his strengths included "superior cognitive abilities, vocabulary and verbal fluency, and general fund of knowledge."

ℕ ℕ ℕ ℕ

John's interest in history had resulted in his being elected to the Mennonite Historical Committee in the summer of 1993. The committee oversees the historical archive for the denomination, which at that point was for only the former Mennonite Church conference, not the former General Conference with which it would later merge to create the present-day Mennonite Church USA and Mennonite Church Canada.

In the fall of 1993, the archives located on the south side of the Goshen College campus in Indiana needed a new director. The job description was lying on the Sharp family's table when MJ came in from school, picked it up, and started reading it. He asked his mom, "Well, did they write this job description before or after they met my dad?"

When Michele asked why, MJ said, "It fits him perfectly."

MJ made it clear he thought John should take the job, but John didn't think that Erin would want to leave Scottdale, where she had formed good friendships and was getting ready to start high school. Michele also wasn't done with schooling she had undertaken in the medical field, and John had another year left in his second three-year term as pastor.

John got the job and they found a house in Middlebury, a small town northeast of Goshen. MJ was "psyched" about a potential move. When his parents told him they were moving, he replied, "Good, we don't belong here anyway." He was getting hassled by his peers at school, and his parents hadn't realized how badly he needed a change.

ﬡ ﬡ ﬡ ﬡ

That summer, as the family transitioned to their new home, they joined thousands of other Mennonites in Wichita, Kansas, for Wichita 95. A Mennonite church convention takes place every other year, gathering adults to tend church business and worship together and youth groups to participate in high-energy worship services. Two years prior, John had officially joined the Historical Committee at the convention in Philadelphia. At Wichita 95, he was the incoming director of the Mennonite Church Historical Committee and Archives. The adult delegates that year were considering a new Mennonite Confession of Faith, updating the one that arose from the Schleitheim Confession of 1527.

Altogether, there were more than 3,200 adults in attendance as well as nearly 4,400 Mennonite teens—including MJ and his sisters—participating in the youth convention. Many youth groups traveled to the youth convention together after raising money from their community or in their church to attend. The growing size of the youth convention was one of the main factors determining where the Mennonite convention would take place. Most of the 1995 event was held in a convention center, but a group of 345 middle school students in grades seven to nine who had come to convention with their families stayed in dorm rooms on the campus of Bethel College in nearby North Newton, Kansas, for their own junior youth convention.

For the preteens, taking over a campus with little supervision was as close to heaven as they could imagine. MJ gained a reputation for putting toothpaste on the back of the doorknobs in the dorm rooms. He met a boy named Andy Gingerich, who became known as "Sugar Boy" for adding packets of sugar to his Mountain Dew. Their parents knew each other, and both families were moving to Middlebury.

Before school started in August, the Sharp family settled into their new home in the Spring Valley subdivision on the west side of town. On the first day of seventh grade, MJ was sitting in a classroom at Heritage Middle School when a dividing wall opened during the last period of the day. He looked over and saw a gangly kid he'd met at the junior youth convention. "Sugar Boy?" MJ called over to Andy Gingerich, who recognized MJ immediately.

As they reconnected at school that day, they realized they lived in the same neighborhood. They didn't share classes, but after school the boys started hanging out, and their friendship quickly blossomed.

At the end of that school year, MJ approached a classmate named Keith Grubaugh on the brief bus ride between school and Spring Valley. "I hear you are the guy to talk to about fishing around here," MJ said to him. Keith saw MJ as popular, smart, and good looking, not to mention confident. They hadn't interacted before, but MJ's reputation had been established in that first year at Heritage.

They made plans for MJ to ride his bike over to Keith's house, which was next door to Andy's, and the three went fishing.

West Lake, the older subdivision to the west of Spring Valley, had three interconnected ponds. At the time, they could easily get to the middle pond and cast from the shore. The summer between seventh and eighth grade was epic for the three boys as they fished with abandon. "I think we literally caught the same fish every day," said Keith.

"I don't know if we directly competed at anything," said Andy, who was most interested in making music and learning

MJ had an affection for fishing his entire life. PHOTO COURTESY JOHN SHARP

guitar. MJ was busy playing soccer in youth leagues. Keith, the shortest and strongest of the three, was becoming a wrestler. Keith's house, which had a pool and vacant lot next to it, became the neighborhood hangout for the three.

"We were the brats of Spring Valley, and to this day, I don't know if the adults in the neighborhood found us impressive or embarrassing," said Andy.

Ŋ Ŋ Ŋ Ŋ

The summer after eighth grade, MJ went exploring, going on major trips that were traditions at schools in northern Indiana.

Over spring break, MJ tagged along on the Goshen High School Marine Biology trip to Florida. Every year in the first week of April, dozens of high school students head to Florida to study marine biology in a course that was developed in large part by Carl Weaver, a longtime GHS science teacher who was also MJ's mentor at Waterford Mennonite Church, where the Sharp family was attending.

Weaver invited MJ to go along. While the high school students were analyzing sea creatures and salt water, MJ fell in with Sarah Yoder and Jed Wulliman, whose parents were teachers at other schools but were helping Carl Weaver with the trip.

"It was the best week ever," said Sarah. They stayed at a rundown lodge with the students and staff where they could get a boat and go fishing, canoeing, or snorkeling. Florida is a respite for many who withstand northern Indiana winters, and the sunshine is a welcome change from gray skies and erratic spring weather. The sunshine was indeed glorious, but Sarah also enjoyed being with MJ. He charmed her on that trip, and she had a major crush on him by the time they boarded the bus to come home.

Yet it was on that trip that MJ also left her with a lesson that lasted far longer than the crush. MJ attended Waterford with Traci Yoder Stoltzfus (née Yoder), who was part of Sarah's small friend group at school. Sarah and three others had turned on Traci, as young people sometimes do, and started teasing her and excluding her.

While they were in Florida, MJ asked Sarah why. "He did it in a way that was in no way accusing me of anything," Sarah remembered. He simply and kindly asked questions. He wanted to know why the relationship was broken. Not many eighth-grade boys could have done what MJ did. Sarah felt deep remorse for abandoning Traci and repaired the relationship when they got back to Indiana. The two remain close friends even as adults nearly twenty-five years later. "Even at thirteen, MJ was doing the work of reconciliation," Sarah said.

When the school year ended, MJ, Andy, and Keith were off on another adventure. Heritage Middle School had started hosting a trip for eighth graders to the Boundary Waters Canoe Area Wilderness. Teachers with a passion for the outdoors and the beautiful million-acre wilderness with thousands of lakes and rivers took several dozen students to northern Minnesota each June.

The trio of friends packed their fishing gear and clothes for several days of paddling canoes on remote lakes and carrying their packs across portage trails as they traversed the wilderness. The students split into groups of six students and two teachers. Andy was in a different group from MJ and Keith, but they all fell in love with the Boundary Waters and the fish stories they could tell, incessantly, between trips.

A month later, MJ and Andy were at Orlando 97, the Mennonite convention. Two years prior they had been part of a junior youth group with organized activities and a sense of ownership. The convention in 1997 wasn't like that.

The junior high students were lumped in with the children while the high school students who were only a little bit older had an entire array of services, workshops, and activities planned just for them. Andy and MJ weren't happy and complained to their parents, who got their boys together. The duo crafted a letter to convention organizers asking for a better experience. "We like to think that we're not children anymore," said the letter they typed together and convinced other middle schoolers to sign. "We also know we aren't [high school] Youth, but we are caught in the middle. . . . We are the future church, and as 7th and 8th graders we have unique needs." They named seminars they would appreciate, including "How to Live a Christian Life Pimples and All." They asked to be challenged about the Bible.

As they worked on the letter, Andy and MJ also talked about their futures, including the possibility of attending Bethany Christian High School together. MJ told his friend that he could picture himself at that school, and they started making plans.

The Dude abides. I don't know about you but I take comfort in that. It's good knowin' he's out there. The Dude. Takin' 'er easy for all us sinners.

—**THE STRANGER** in *The Big Lebowski*

FOUR

For Whom the Bell Tolls

THOUGH IT MEANT leaving Keith, Andy and MJ both decided to go to Bethany Christian High School.

The Sharp family had just moved a dozen miles away to Goshen since MJ's older sister Erin was attending Goshen High School. John's work was there, and Michele had also found a job there as a medical assistant.

Keith stayed at Northridge, where he could be on the wrestling team. As a small private school, Bethany didn't offer as many sports, including wrestling, swimming, and football, as the Indiana public schools did. Bethany did have Bible classes in the curriculum, a focus on relationships among the students and staff, and—of particular interest to MJ— a well-established soccer team.

MJ's first identity at Bethany was as a jock—someone who played sports and attracted attention from young women. He was dating Sarah Yoder, whom he'd met on the marine biology trip to Florida, and making friends as he studied computer applications and environmental science and joined the chorale with Andy. At Heritage, MJ had earned nearly straight As. A B-plus in German, a language he would eventually speak and write fluently, prompted his father to write a letter to the teacher inquiring how MJ could have improved his work to receive an A. As MJ entered Bethany, he said his goal was to keep a 4.0 GPA and play basketball, soccer, and baseball.

He never ended up going out for baseball and he never had a semester with straight As, much less eight semesters strung together. His freshman year, he mostly had A-minuses with a few Bs and B-pluses, including a B-plus in the second semester of geometry. It wasn't that he couldn't do the work. MJ was brilliant, and those around him knew it, though, he didn't try to flaunt it. He was just bored much of the time at school. While he was in a geometry class he really didn't enjoy, he looked up at the seventy-four digits of pi—the infinitely continuing mathematical constant—that the teacher had posted encircling the room and memorized all seventy-four digits, and likely far more beyond that.

ון וו וו וו

After MJ got his license, he told John he wanted to drive a sports car. John had a motorcycle, and at Michele's urging he agreed to give up riding and sell the bike. MJ found a 1983 Porsche 944 online, and with proceeds from the sale of the motorcycle and another family car, they had enough to buy it. John bought his son a plane ticket, and they planned for MJ to fly to Philadelphia and then hitchhike to the owner's house in New Jersey. After test-driving the car, he paid for it and drove it home to Indiana. Joel Koeneman, a high school friend, helped MJ install the shocks and brakes it needed. The car ran well, and MJ loved it.

MJ cleans a beloved Porsche at his home in Goshen. PHOTO COURTESY JOHN SHARP

He loved anything that was well-designed, but what teenager wouldn't love a car with power and speed? The straight, open roads of Indiana don't offer many opportunities for tight cornering, but they do allow a driver to punch the accelerator and see how fast something will go.

After MJ's sister Laura got hit by a Cadillac while driving MJ's beloved Porsche (something he had fiercely protested), the family bought another Porsche, which they had for a few years before they bought a minivan from the Gingerich family for a dollar. That vehicle, dubbed "the Andy Van," stayed in the Sharp family for years.

₪ ₪ ₪ ₪

Bethany students take part in interterm, a week during which students take a class on campus or leave campus for a for-credit experience. MJ went canoe camping his freshman year and joined "Living in Christian Community," working at a camp in southern Indiana, his sophomore year. Jen Myers (née Gingerich), a friend from school and church, was along on that trip as her father neared death at home from pancreatic cancer.

MJ checked on her to make sure she was doing okay, as he also did in the hallways or cafeteria at school in ways that their classmates didn't. "For me, he brought a lot of genuine care, but lightheartedness, to situations," she said.

His leadership at the camp shaped the group, and during a candlelit closing service in the lodge, Bible teacher Dale Shenk carried out the priestly function of blessing each student. "What came out when MJ knelt in front of me was, 'You have incredible potential,'" Dale said. It was an intentional two-sided comment, since Dale knew what young MJ was capable of yet also knew that Bethany teachers hadn't always seen MJ at his best.

MJ's reputation of being smart but not engaged led English teacher Suzanne Ehst to misread a paper he submitted on *The Color Purple*. MJ had used sarcasm to point out how important the book and its themes were, but Suzanne read his tone as dismissive of the gender and abuse issues raised in Alice Walker's classic novel. She saw his crestfallen look as she handed him back his paper with the low grade, and she sought him out in the hallway after class. She asked if she had misunderstood and he said yes, explaining that he thought it was dumb not to take such issues seriously. She apologized and changed the grade.

"He was both so delightful to teach and so frustrating at the same time," she said.

While giving a persuasive speech in his junior year, MJ ditched the outline and research he had submitted in preparation. He instead stood in front of the class and told them he would bend the spoon he was holding with his mind. His classmates were entertained as he stared at the spoon, his face shaking. Suzanne and the students were convinced that MJ would indeed bend the spoon. The speech had worked, though Suzanne wasn't sure how to grade the stunt.

After one of MJ's high school report cards had come home, John told his son he was underperforming and urged him to work toward getting the good grades that would assure college. John warned MJ that if he kept goofing off, he'd be on his own to pay for college.

The problem wasn't MJ's intelligence. He continued to score well on tests, including the SAT, on which he missed a perfect math score by one question. The strong test scores helped his college applications, but his grades didn't.

While MJ didn't flaunt his brilliance, he wasn't unaware of it, either. His friend Joel once asked him, "Do you ever get the feeling you could be a genius but you're not sure?"

MJ said, "Yeah, the only difference is I know I'm a genius." He told Joel that his IQ was in the 160 range, which if true would have put him in rare space in the world. Less than 0.1 percent of people have an IQ above 145, and those with an IQ of 160 include the late physicists Stephen Hawking and Albert Einstein.

ℕ ℕ ℕ ℕ

In a Mennonite family that wasn't wealthy and prized hard work, MJ often had a job. What he wanted along with the income was to be learning or excelling at something.

As a second grader, MJ had gone door-to-door selling from a catalog of items on behalf of his older sister Erin, who was in fifth grade. She became the top salesperson in the school fundraiser, thanks to MJ, and got the see-through phone with neon wires that she wanted as her prize.

When he was thirteen, his first job was selling vacuum cleaners, or as he was instructed to call them, "cleaning systems." Keith's father and stepmother Tom and Barb sat through one of the first presentations after MJ had been trained. His efforts to sell the vacuums were short-lived, but his presentations impressed even those who didn't buy one, including the Grubaughs.

Starting when he was fourteen, he washed dishes at a restaurant and later in high school learned retail service and other tasks at Snyder Paints, a family-owned store in Goshen. A collection of characters, including contractors and landlords buying paint, taught him how to solve problems and a number of other lessons. MJ learned from a coworker who had been a policeman how to challenge a speeding ticket—a helpful tool when driving a Porsche.

MJ went to work for a prominent local landlord and learned property maintenance, which led MJ and a realtor friend, Jeff Birky, to buy two properties each with two units. MJ was a landlord while he was in high school and college.

One Christmas break during college, MJ discovered a bathroom faucet in one of the units that wouldn't shut off and called a plumber, but when the resident said he would take care of it, MJ opted to let him. When MJ came home months later, the renters were gone and the water was still flowing. He owed the city more than $3,000 for the water bill. The city wouldn't back down, so MJ gulped hard and paid the bill.

ᓂ ᓂ ᓂ ᓂ

In MJ's senior yearbook, color photos of the seniors are accompanied by their Myers-Briggs Type Indicator (ENTJ for MJ) and words or phrases that describe them. MJ is noted for being intelligent, logical, and witty. But the yearbook also notes what he is best remembered for at Bethany.

In the late 1990s, as dial-up internet started to connect high schoolers to the world in different ways, MJ hit the information superhighway. He loved gadgets and technology and was quick to adopt both.

In the fall of his junior year, MJ posed as a scientific researcher and persuaded a purveyor to mail him live mice, which became the bit actors in an elaborate prank.

Bethany has a long tradition of seniors pulling a prank at the school. Teachers and administrators are generally patient with the efforts of seventeen- and eighteen-year-olds who want to be clever, as long as the resulting mess can be cleaned up quickly. The pranks often happen in the spring, effectively serving as a pressure valve for teenagers ready for the school year and their high school careers to be over.

In the fall and early winter of 1999, the question of what would happen when January 1, 2000, arrived was on the minds of many Americans, and MJ and several junior classmates seized the opportunity to orchestrate a prank and blame it on the senior class. On December 27, over the holiday break when few were in the building, they broke into the school with the live mice MJ had ordered online. They placed the rodents in desk drawers and even put some in the tiles of the drop ceiling. They supplied the mice with birdseed to help them survive until students and staff returned.

The group used the library photocopier to make copies of a poster that Andy had designed in Microsoft Paint with a mouse holding "2000." They also made the image a screensaver on computers throughout the building. A twelve-line poem on the poster spoke of the prank that would go down in history and was written as if seniors of the class of 2000 were doing the prank before Y2K hit so that it would be well-remembered.

What MJ, Andy, and others didn't realize was how much damage a few mice can do, even if they are contained in small places. Despite having taken biology, the boys didn't understand how quickly mice can reproduce.

As school resumed for the second semester, the seniors weren't pleased to be blamed for a prank they didn't enact, but it wasn't clear who had actually done it. The mood in the school was tense. Keith, who attended a different school, had offhandedly told the story, including who was responsible, to one of his wrestling teammates. That person told a Bethany senior at a poker gathering. "I never thought my hooligan wrestling buddies at Northridge would have any connection to my good Christian buddies at Bethany," Keith said.

Word traveled, and juniors were soon brought in for questioning by school officials. Nick Gingerich, Andy's cousin and one of the perpetrators, cracked first. On January 6, the assistant principal told the boys that they'd each pay twelve dollars to cover the cost of ceiling tiles and photocopying from when they broke in to the library, help set up and take down chairs at graduation, pay for the replacement of some locks, and spend eight hours on a Saturday helping the groundskeeper. They were also told they couldn't participate in the senior prank the next year and had to apologize to the seniors.

When MJ stood in front of the seniors gathered in the chapel during a lunch period, he apologized on behalf of the group, as the administrators had instructed. The seniors gave him a standing ovation.

MJ's thinking was that if they did a prank their junior year, they would get two pranks during their high school career rather than just one. Though they were instructed not to do a prank their senior year, it didn't stop MJ and Andy from forming a new team the next fall. They simply used what they learned and were more careful this time.

In basement strategy sessions, they planned to use the intercom in creative ways to mimic an administrator, but once they were in the school office at night they discovered another opportunity. As they worked around the old intercom system, they realized that the back of the bell system module had a switch override. Crossing two of the wires attached to it made the bells ring. "That was very exciting for seniors in high school. Quite a power trip," said Andy.

Wires from the intercom system traveled throughout the building to speakers. The boys bought identical colored wire and installed two strands through the harnesses and ceiling and into an empty, unused locker for which they'd found the combination in the office.

MJ led the operation, patiently and with tactical finesse.

At first, one of the team would get out of class and, after assuring that no one was watching, touch the wires together at the locker a few minutes before the end of class to trigger the school bells. Over the following weeks, the bells rang again and again at random times, causing confusion among students and educators. Joel Koeneman remembers seeing MJ at the locker in the hallway one day, and MJ gave his friend a huge, cheesy, and mischievous grin before he crossed the wires.

One time the wires crossed in the locker without anyone touching them together, and the bell rang for minutes. The boys were in various classes throughout the building and were also puzzled by the long ringing. In Andy's study hall, the teacher exclaimed, "This system's just crap." It was several minutes until MJ could get to the locker to stop the ringing.

School officials were baffled. They couldn't figure out how it was happening and brought in someone to service the system. John had stopped by the Bethany office one morning and overheard administrators say they might have to buy a new system and that it would likely cost thousands of dollars. Many suspected that MJ was somehow behind the bells ringing, including MJ's sister Laura, who was a sophomore at Bethany.

As a father, John had boiled down his set of rules to three simple ones for his sharp son: Don't break anything. If you do break it, pay for it. And never lie about anything.

John went home that night and told MJ, "The jig is up."

MJ walked across the street to his neighbor's house. Peter Shetler, who lived across the street from the Sharps, was in charge of building maintenance and some of the school's technology. Peter had been working to figure out the problem, but he had been at the school only a few months and hadn't yet been able to resolve the issue. As Peter remembers it, the school was getting ready to hire consultants to find the problem.

MJ tried to offer a solution while also assuring protection for his classmates and himself. He asked Peter, "If I told you how to fix the bells, would anyone have to know about it?"

The pranks were one of the few things that still gave MJ energy at high school. He was interested in learning, just not his classes. He graduated with a 3.12 GPA and ranked twentieth in a graduating class of fifty-three.

₪ ₪ ₪ ₪

As MJ's senior year approached, he begged his parents to let him leave Bethany Christian. He had enough credits to graduate. The Sharps agreed that MJ could join his uncle and aunt Dave and Pat Sharp, who were missionaries to Indigenous people in the jungles of Costa Rica. MJ would spend the last semester of high school in Costa Rica rather than in classes.

MJ's grandfather Mahlon flew with him from Chicago to San José, where MJ joined his uncle and aunt for nearly three months. MJ had studied Spanish since the beginning of his time at Bethany, and he went with a thirst for adventure and tools, including his father's nice camera, twenty rolls of film, and a journal he dubbed "Wilson," after the volleyball Tom Hanks talked to in the movie *Castaway*. MJ filled the pages of that journal with his tiny script, listing the words he'd learned in Spanish that day by trial and error. "*Revelar* is the word of the day," he wrote on January 25, 2001, three days after arriving in the country. "It means 'to develop' as in pictures. This word would have been very helpful to know when I tried to explain that I wanted my film developed. Instead of using the word *revelar*, I used the words eh, err and umm."

In nearly daily entries, he would list his status on a scale of one to ten in categories of health, boredom, Spanish proficiency, and homesickness. That last number stayed relatively low, but he did write about how much he missed his dog D'Artagnan and the way he would "wash my face and ears at night," he wrote.

While in Costa Rica, MJ traveled with his aunt and uncle, attending church services and working at churches or with people doing construction or farming. He fished often with members of his host family or others in the town, but instead of using a rod and reel, he fired a spear at the fish.

He went on adventures, climbing an active volcano, rafting whitewater rapids, and regularly swimming in the river. He got sick a couple of times, but mostly took the challenges of living in a foreign country in stride. He prayed earnestly and wrote of feeling close to God. As he encountered a different culture and even other Mennonites who saw faith and how it intersected with the world very differently, he responded graciously. "It is my belief that you can never be beyond salvation since the two thieves on either side of Jesus on the cross repented and were saved," he wrote.

His parents relayed the admissions decisions arriving in letters from colleges and universities, and he wrestled with the question of where to enroll. He was most drawn to Eastern Mennonite University, with Goshen College as a backup. His grade point average at Bethany kept him from getting the President's Scholarship or Honors Scholarship at EMU that would have covered much of the cost of college. The Honors College at the University of Pittsburgh offered him a full-tuition scholarship, but he hadn't enjoyed the campus when he had visited the school near where he'd spent his elementary years. He joked about leaving out a fleece the way Gideon had in the Old Testament, only his would have been candy representing EMU or Pitt for ants to choose. By late March, he wrote in his journal, "God: please help me find a way to go to EMU. It's clearly where I feel You calling me to go."

His parents still had debt from their own schooling, and he calculated how much debt he might have at college graduation. "I might have to gamble to pay for my education," he wrote.

He never did get his ATM card to work in Costa Rica, but one day in early March he took $15 in cash to a casino in San José, "I just had to see if I could win at blackjack the way I could on the computer," he wrote. He had memorized the times when one should hit in the game, when to double down, how to play the odds. With the charts in his head, he sat at a casino table for the first time. Within an hour, this eighteen-year-old gringo drinking free Pepsis left with $155 tucked in his sock.

After an hour in his hotel room, he realized he was bored and went back with $30. He doubled that in half an hour, and another man at the table who was also winning steadily started offering advice on strategy and even counting cards. The man asked MJ why he was afraid to lose when he was doing so well, and MJ started betting $5 a hand rather than $1.50. When they cashed in their chips, MJ had watched the man win at least $500, while MJ had won more than $300 and drank a lot of free Pepsi.

He confessed some guilt in his journal, but said he'd keep thinking about it and that he enjoyed playing. He wrote, "I don't win based on luck, although it helps, I win because I've studied the game."

₪ ₪ ₪ ₪

After a successful stint as an international traveler, MJ returned to Goshen. He had learned the language and eaten like the locals. He had worked to understand their culture and celebrate it.

Back in Goshen, he spent time with his friends and on their new hobby: bowling. The movie *The Big Lebowski* had been released in 1998 when Keith, Andy, and MJ were freshmen. It may be the best bowling movie of all time, in which the Dude, as Jeff Bridges's character is known, is involved in a case of mistaken identity and is targeted by those who believe he's responsible for kidnapping a wealthy man's wife. In reality, the Dude is just a guy who loves White Russian cocktails, a rug that is ruined early on in the movie, and smoking marijuana. And he loves his friends Walter and Donny. The quirky movie, written and directed by Ethan Coen and Joel Coen, became a cult classic for many, including Keith, Andy, MJ and a handful of other friends. Andy saw the movie on VHS after school one day at a friend's home and soon showed it to his friends. They then watched the movie regularly and went bowling. Over time, lines from the movie became a regular part of their banter:

"The Dude abides."

"The Dude minds. This will not stand, ya know, this aggression will not stand, man."

"Sometimes there's a man . . . I won't say a hero, 'cause, what's a hero? But sometimes, there's a man. And I'm talkin' about the Dude here. Sometimes, there's a man, well, he's the man for his time and place. He fits right in there. And that's the Dude."

As these teens graduated from high school, life was full of possibility. MJ, Andy, and Keith were often up to something, but they were also totally comfortable just hanging out. They would drive, MJ behind the wheel, windows down. The cool Indiana air carried the smell of ripening corn. And something funny had just happened or was about to happen.

Inspection stickers used to have printed on the back, "Drive carefully: the life you save may be your own." That is the wisdom of men in a nutshell. What God says, on the other hand, is, "The life you save is the life you lose." In other words, the life you clutch, hoard, guard, and play safe with is in the end a life worth little to anybody, including yourself; and only a life given away for love's sake is a life worth living. To bring this point home, God shows us a man who gave his life away to the extent of dying a national disgrace without a penny in the bank or a friend to his name. In terms of men's wisdom, he was a perfect fool, and anybody who thinks he can follow him without making something like the same kind of fool of himself is laboring not under a cross but a delusion.

—FREDERICK BUECHNER, *Wishful Thinking*

FIVE

Pushing Buttons and Playing Chips

IN THE FALL OF 2001, after going fishing with Andy and Keith one more time, after one last viewing of *The Big Lebowski*, MJ headed to Eastern Mennonite University in the Shenandoah Valley of Virginia.

As he had said in Costa Rica, he wanted God to help him find a way to go to EMU. He had reached out to Judy Mullet, a professor of education and later psychology, who oversaw the honors program that would have offered standing and scholarship money.

She was recruiting students for the program, and though his grade point average wasn't good enough to get him in, she engaged him in conversation. "He's just the kind of person we want at EMU," she said.

She noted that he was philosophical and had a passion for social justice and urged him to go to a place that would nurture him in areas that interested him and could grab his attention.

As Andy headed to Bethel College and Keith stayed home to work for two years, MJ was going to EMU in Harrisonburg. As one of the communities in the United States where Mennonites had originally settled to farm, Harrisonburg also has a sizable Anabaptist population, including Old Order Mennonites in the outlying areas. The community also has a number of Mennonite churches along with a Mennonite high school.

MJ moved into the Roselawn dorm, sharing a room with Jason Garber from Kansas. On move-in weekend, their moms wiped out cabinets in the small room as the young men set up their massive computer systems on desks underneath their loft beds.

MJ entered college with eighteen credits in Spanish, college algebra, and macroeconomics. Having a semester's worth of college credits was huge for a young person paying his way through college. MJ declared a history major, which pleased his father. John and Michele had followed through on the warning about MJ's high school grades and told MJ he would pay for college on his own, though they were helping Erin with her tuition at Goshen College. They helped with incidentals, but he was responsible for paying tuition, room, and board.

On the first day of classes that fall, he and classmate Rachel Jenner (née Swartzendruber) noticed a typographical error in the syllabus for Introduction to Politics. The professor, who was new on campus, had written "public policy" without the letter *l* in *public*. The teenagers giggled at the inadvertent reference to an area of the body.

Rachel had grown up Mennonite in Indianapolis and was starting her college career as well. MJ lived on the second floor of Roselawn dorm with Jason, and she lived on the third floor.

She was intrigued by him and enjoyed how he made this class together more tolerable. They started using Instant Messenger to communicate when they weren't together.

She soon had a crush on this guy who was, in her words, "really stinking smart," but also funny and genuine. He made the first move and was soon courting her.

He wasn't a "good Mennonite boy" like those she had encountered before. He wasn't just following the traditional path. He'd skipped the last semester of high school and was learning how to play online poker. He had gotten a lockpicking set and was teaching himself how to use it. Yet he was strong in his Christian convictions.

By Thanksgiving, they were a couple. "For us, it meant a lot of just hanging out in each other's rooms and joining friend's circles a little bit," she said. Yet when they went on a date, he would put energy and focus on her. "If he wanted something, if he was going to go on a date with you, he was really going to try," she said.

On Sunday mornings, the couple would ride in MJ's car to one of the local Mennonite churches to enjoy the pancake breakfast provided to college students before the service and then go out to eat afterward.

Life was good that fall. MJ earned straight As in his classes. He got along with his roommate. In the dorm, the students would play the word game Scrabble. "Basically it would be everybody versus MJ," said Jason. He was usually much better than any of them.

MJ had his own meticulous approach to things. He enjoyed having a powerful computer on his desk and a fast internet connection and spent hours online learning about all sorts of things.

He told Jason that he wanted to get into vermiculture and use worms to compost food scraps. Soon after, a box labeled

"Live Nude Worms" arrived in the campus post office in the Campus Center, and MJ put the thousand red invertebrates in plastic tubs and fed them food scraps. As the young men left for Christmas break, MJ had learned from his research that they could survive for several weeks without feedings. What he didn't anticipate was that their room, which was often so warm they had to open their window to regulate the temperature, wouldn't have any heat during the break between semesters. When they returned to campus in January, the worms had frozen to death.

₪ ₪ ₪ ₪

In his college classes, MJ loved to amp up discussions, but not by attacking others. He would listen carefully to his classmates and then counter their viewpoints. "He liked to argue for the sake of arguing. He loved being devil's advocate," said Mark Metzler Sawin, who had just joined the faculty as a new history professor.

MJ would sometimes burst into the offices of professors as he sought their counsel. Judy Mullet never taught him in class, but in those first two years of college, he would come talk to her about his courses and other aspects of life. He was at times discouraged because he couldn't make himself do some of the work that needed to be done. He talked with her about how he had trouble concentrating and finishing things that didn't grab his attention. Yet in that first year of college, the only B he got was in his second biology class. The rest were As.

Rachel saw MJ when he was full of energy and also when he was huddled in his room playing online poker. She rode in his Porsche, sometimes singing show tunes with him. One Sunday, on the way back from church in the Porsche, MJ decided he wanted to hit a hundred miles an hour on Route 42, a local highway. Rachel protested. He assured her it would be fine, and they argued until she realized she didn't have a choice. She saw that what he was doing seemed out of bounds, but that if anyone was going to do it and be fine, it was MJ.

Though they had wonderful times together in a year and a half of dating, the second semester of their sophomore year took its toll on MJ and Rachel. They had gone on spring break to Florida together, but MJ's insisting on hitchhiking rather than riding with her had caused tension between them. They were working closely over long hours in the office of the campus newspaper, the *Weather Vane*. They were arguing over random things and would both dig in on their positions.

MJ and Rachel had dated for nearly all their college experience so far and now it was over. The end of a dating relationship on a small college campus puts strain on the friendships that surround them as well as on the individuals involved. Rachel struggled over the coming weeks. MJ ended the semester with a C in an English class and a C-plus in speech. He withdrew from Church History and got no credit. His only A was for his role on the *Weather Vane*.

ꗍ ꗍ ꗍ ꗍ

MJ became a journalist while in college as a way to channel his growing passions for justice, equity, and making a difference.

In January 2003, the second semester of his sophomore year, he'd become an editor of the *Weather Vane*, the weekly student newspaper. That semester and the fall of his junior year he was in leadership with others of the newspaper and did hard-hitting stories about news on campus, including a scandal with a women's basketball coach. His writing on national and international politics also drew criticism from some on campus, who said leadership of the paper was failing to give voice to the "silent majority."

In January 2004, MJ had taken the semester off and was in Goshen, recouping from the rough fall semester.

He wrote a piece for *The Agora*, an independent, student-run alternative blog launched by his cohort of EMU journalists, in March 2004 about not having wanted to leave college and planning to return when he saved up enough money. He had gone back to work for the Goshen landlord again, and one day he went out with two veterans of foreign wars to collect rent. When a tenant came out with a Louisville Slugger aluminum bat, one of the vets took it from him and used it to break the man's kneecaps, he wrote.

As he encountered very different thoughts and approaches to solving problems, MJ found ways to engage others in conversation. He asked one of the veterans about why he always carried a gun, and Harold told MJ that his grandfather had told him two things. "Number one, there's nothing worse than needing a gun and not having one. Number two, an unloaded gun never does anyone a lick of good." MJ said that as a good Mennonite who had read Mennonite peace theology and learned quite different lessons about guns from his grandfather Mahlon, he tried to make a case for nonviolence, but it didn't hold up with Harold.

As MJ worked in Goshen, he distanced himself from college life. "He suffered. It cost him," said Judy Mullet. In an email exchange that spring, the two of them discussed the alienation he felt over how people had responded to his work on the newspaper. And he expressed hope about a new business venture he and Jason Garber were planning.

The two had worked together well in a range of ways, including on an epic prank effort in the fall of 2003, their junior year. MJ gathered Jason and others to help rewrite a new university hymn the night before it was to be sung for the first time at the Homecoming Weekend opening chapel service.

Using a computer, they changed the song lyrics subtly. "Christ of the desert" became "Christ of the dessert." "Jesus our teacher friend" became "Jesus our T-shirt friend."

His friends made copies as he hid in the auditorium so they could get in to replace the song sheets.

The changes were discovered the next morning and the original text was the one sung, not their version. "He came back dejected," said Jason.

Jason and MJ were going to purchase Segway scooters, the two-wheeled, battery-powered vehicles that were beginning to grow in popularity since launching just a few years before, and use them to give tours in Washington, D.C. "If this works out at all, I'll have plenty of money for the rest of my undergrad and a lot of law school," he told Judy. Though Jason and MJ had worked out a business plan, MJ said he clearly planned to return to EMU.

The venture would have combined energetically engaging customers on new technology that fascinated MJ, who was poised to be the manager. Jason made a bid on a commercial property near the National Mall, but the landlord rejected their offer and tried to advise them against starting the business. Jason pulled the plug on the venture and MJ was left coping with the disappointment and seeking other ways to pay for college.

בּ בּ בּ בּ

There was always poker.

The books he read, and the time he spent on PartyPoker.com, began to pay off. He didn't always win, but he won enough to help pay his bills and continue to play. The losses, if you can call them that, included the college papers he didn't finish on time and the classes he missed.

MJ would talk his way toward some sort of agreement with the professors of the classes that were boring him. He could talk his way into or out of anything. "He just knew how to reason with people wherever they were at," said Clinton Miller, a college friend and roommate.

MJ learned how to play Texas Hold'em, a game simple enough for nearly anyone to play and enjoy, but also layered with beauty and complexity so that students of the game can win more than they lose by playing the cards they're dealt and the others at the table. The odds change with each card dealt, and having a sense of the percentages, as MJ did in his head, can reduce the luck needed to rake in a big pot.

When MJ turned twenty-one in October 2003, he drove to Atlantic City, the coastal New Jersey city with a long history of casino gambling. Though MJ appeared to be young and innocent, he had a poker face. He found himself in a game with a professional player who he knew was underestimating him.

He bluffed. And won. And came back to campus with several thousand dollars.

There's no way of knowing how many hours MJ spent playing poker in college, but as he earned money that helped pay for his formal schooling, he was also learning about risk and reward and how the two are intertwined. By his senior year of college, MJ had acquired his own set of poker chips. He brought them to a weekly game with other students and recent graduates. Classmate Ben Wideman was part of the game with MJ and saw him as "a half-step cooler than I was." Though MJ was relaxed in that friendly game, Ben learned that he didn't want to be in a showdown with him either.

When MJ was playing poker, MJ understood the risks and potential reward and could balance them so that he won more than he lost.

ℶ ℶ ℶ ℶ

MJ's senior history project, inspired by Tony Horwitz's 1998 book *Confederates in the Attic*, focused on Mennonites living in the Shenandoah Valley during the US Civil War.

In the twenty-page paper titled "Closet Confederates: Pockets of Southern Sentiment among Shenandoah Valley Mennonites," MJ told of how three hundred to four hundred Mennonite families in the valley navigated the fighting of the Union and Confederate forces. "They were known as good citizens, who abided by the laws, paid taxes, and farmed the land well," MJ wrote, drawing on the histories he studied and cited.

Some Mennonites fled north to avoid being forced to fight in the military. Others paid a fine and avoided conscription. The position of not fighting in the war wasn't a popular one and had costs for many Anabaptists. One Brethren elder named John Kline, responding to warnings about plots to kill him, said, "I am threatened: they may take my life; but I do not fear them; they can only kill the body." Kline was murdered for trying to secure safety for religious objectors. MJ also cited the story of Christ Good, who was in the Confederate Army but refused to shoot the Yankees, telling a captain, "They're people. We don't shoot people."

MJ's interviews with Mennonites who had ancestors in the valley during the war uncovered support for the Confederacy and secession. In the conclusion of the paper, MJ pointed out that some talked whimsically about the South and its great generals. Though in the minority, they would pass on their convictions to the next generation, he said. In his paper, MJ showed that Mennonite thought and practice isn't uniform across groups, and that how peace and pacifism is viewed and practiced varies. That was a valuable lens through which to view his own commitment to pacifism.

Like many seniors in college, he had by his final year outgrown campus and was ready to move on. His college career hadn't gone as he'd expected. His final grade point average was a respectable 3.19, though it was clear he could have gotten better grades if he had worked at his classes as he had poker and pranks.

Instead of heading to law school, MJ applied for an opening through Mennonite Mission Network for a position working with soldiers seeking conscientious objector status in Germany. That would take him overseas and put him in a position to both practice peacemaking and work in a foreign language.

In her reference on his behalf, Judy Mullet touted how he thrived on risks as demonstrated by his time as editor of the *Weather Vane*. She had never had him in class, but she had maintained a mentoring friendship and often saw him at Lindale Mennonite Church, where she attended.

Judy described him as "open minded, outspoken, yet sensitive to alternative perspectives." She named that he sometimes struggled to work consistently on anything he "doesn't believe in with his whole being."

Mennonite Mission Network, at which Michele Sharp had worked in the early 1980s when it was called Mennonite Board of Missions, had been sending Mennonites into the world to do evangelism, service, or relief work since 1899. Now it was sending MJ.

MJ delights in a platter of sushi. PHOTO
COURTESY JOHN SHARP

Put your sword back! These are the last words—a definitive rebuke—the disciples hear from Jesus before they run away. If ever there was a moment in God's eyes when violence would be justifiable, this is it! But Jesus is clear: Put your sword back! His followers are not allowed to respond with violence. They are not allowed to kill. They are not allowed to harm others. They are not allowed to threaten others. They are not permitted to "deter" violent crime with the use of violence.

—**JOHN DEAR**, *Jesus the Rebel*

SIX

Swords into Plowshares

WHEN MJ ARRIVED in Bammental, Germany, in August 2005, he was armed with a stack of books, a firm grasp of the German language, and zeal for a new adventure. American Mennonites, mostly men, have historically served as volunteers domestically and across the world to avoid military service. The mission board placed volunteers in "international ministries" to support programs in Germany, Great Britain, and Nepal. That work often focused on mediation and assisting churches or organizations such as the Peace Committee. The Military Counseling Network (MCN), as part of the Peace Committee, was created so that volunteers such as MJ could walk along-side and counsel American GIs stationed in Germany on their rights, military regulations, and procedures, including applying for conscientious objection.

From 1950 to 2000, more than ten million US soldiers were stationed in Germany, more than any other foreign country by a wide margin.[1] A number of American bases are in the southern region of the country near Bammental. As a new century started, around seventy thousand American troops were stationed there and going to and from active combat in the Middle East and Afghanistan.

The MCN program wasn't always active as part of the Peace Committee's work, but was reestablished after the US invasion of Iraq in 2003. More soldiers were interested in conversations about how to opt out of the military and its violent approach to trying to solve the world's problems.

David Stutzman, who had graduated from Eastern Mennonite University in 2000 and gone to Germany in 2002, needed a new volunteer to work with him in MCN. MJ arrived to help. They worked in a small room in the Peace Committee office in an old building near the small city's center.

A few months shy of his twenty-third birthday, MJ was learning a new role and becoming "Michael," which was easier to say for speakers of languages other than English.

MJ got to live and sometimes work in the German language he had learned in college and practiced during his previous European travels. Soon he was reading *War and Peace* in German. He had loved the English translation of the novel by Leo Tolstoy about the French invasion of Russia and now was tackling it in a second language.

Bammental is a small town near Heidelberg in southwestern Germany where Mennonites have lived and worked since the mid-1980s. Wolfgang Krauss, a historian who was part of the Deutsche Mennonitisches Friedenskomitee (German Mennonite Peace Committee, also known as DMFK), established a permanent office in October 1984 and got volunteers from the United States to come and help the work of promoting and building peace in Germany.

Both David and MJ lived at Hausgemeinschaft, an intentional community in Bammental, with various employees of the Peace Committee and others who had roles in town. All of them committed to living together simply in small rooms or apartments in two buildings located about a ten-minute walk from the Peace Committee office and across from the Reilsheim train station. More than seventy people have lived at Hausgemeinschaft over the past four decades, and numerous others have received the warm hospitality extended to visitors.

In a common kitchen, community members take turns preparing lunch for each other six days a week. Usually one person cooks for the others who live there, which ranges from four to twenty at any given time, and two others wash dishes.

"We live together. We share a meal at one o'clock," said Wolfgang Krauss, who continues to serve as one of the leaders of Hausgemeinschaft. On Sunday nights, the group gathers for a community meeting in which they process their lives together. They sit on furniture accumulated over the years, amid posters and wall hangings that found their way to this spot from around the world. This version of shabby chic illustrates the thriftiness of Mennonites and their wish to make where they live feel like home, no matter where they are from.

Once a month or so they work together on the two buildings or in the garden that is in the courtyard along with an apple tree and cherry tree. On nice days, the group eats on the patio outside the kitchen, passing food family style and pouring glasses of water for each other.

Michael, as he had come to be known in this community, took his turns cooking for the dozen or so people who lived at Hausgemeinschaft then. In addition to running and playing basketball in the courtyard, he had a new health-related focus at the time. He was set on avoiding carbohydrates. Though the low-carb movement had been alive and well in the United States for more than a decade, it was an unlikely nutritional path in Germany. He introduced the concept to those around him, and they remember how diligently he avoided carbs when he was the cook. Yet most of their memories of MJ are not what he was leaving out but what he added to their community and how they understood the work of peacemaking.

ℵ ℵ ℵ ℵ

When David Stutzman arrived in Germany in 2002 as part of German Mennonite Voluntary Service, he didn't have much to do. The Cold War that had occasioned the program was over, and he had little opportunity to use his justice, peace and conflict studies major from EMU. Instead, he played games on the computer. He played so much that he once won a hundred games in a row of FreeCell solitaire.

But in the wake of 9/11, the march to war began. In the fall of 2001, the United States military invaded Afghanistan. By March 2003, it had invaded Iraq. The thousands of service members in Germany were being called into action. The Deutsche Mennonitisches Friedenskomitee rebooted the Military Counseling Network, and David went to work. He was trained on how to counsel GIs on their rights. His first call was from a soldier going to Iraq who was unsure of his willingness to fight.

David learned about the wars, the military, and the day-to-day life of a soldier. One other person had worked alongside him briefly before MJ arrived in 2005.

MJ was so glad to undertake the work. "He was just fresh-faced and energetic and excited to be there," said David.

Many North American Mennonites, consciously or otherwise, look down on the military and reject its principles—an outgrowth of their pacifist beliefs that nations should use nonviolent means to solve disputes. Others who aren't strictly pacifist but choose nonresistance, simply saying that they won't fight but perhaps others can or should, also don't have a reason to engage the military or how it operates. But MJ was willing to step into and live with the tension of believing in pacifism while relating to those who disagreed.

Soldiers would call David and MJ at the office or on their rudimentary cell phones and ask to meet. Because talking to a soldier who might be interested in going absent without leave (AWOL) wouldn't be appropriate in the barracks, they often arranged meetings in coffee shops or bars. Sometimes, the soldiers were serious about not fighting because of a growing conviction. Other times they were simply regretting what they'd signed up to do. David mentored MJ as he learned how to understand and respond to the various reasons that brought soldiers to MCN.

Another mentoring friendship came from within the military structure itself.

Robert Evers had grown up in Nebraska and joined the US Navy out of high school in 1989. After a stint on a battleship, he left active duty for Arizona, where he got married, had a son, got divorced, and dropped out of school. After bouncing around, he joined the US Army in 2001 and was stationed in Germany on September 11.

In the aftermath of 9/11, Robert deployed to Kosovo. He was part of a division that was one of a huge movement of US troops from Kuwait through Baghdad. He was terrified, but he survived.

On a whim, he called MCN one day. He met MJ and David and enjoyed the conversation, but realized he was still willing to be a soldier. As MJ and David continued to navigate the command structure of the military and those who no longer wanted to be part of it, Sgt. Bob became a key ally. Not only could the military man teach the young Mennonites about military weaponry, but he could help them determine whether someone was serious about taking on the consequences of not fighting, and if so, how to help the soldier.

Sgt. Bob would ask if MJ and David had filled out a proper form. He could tell them if the person's rights were being abused by commanding officers after they did so. Sgt. Bob liked MJ and David and was willing to help. The soldier and MJ would trade books and discuss them. They read Mark Twain, renegade travel journalist Robert Young Pelton, and historical fiction novels about wars.

It was a friendship that lasted the rest of MJ's life.

ℶ ℶ ℶ ℶ

In Bammental, MJ quickly forged friendships and was at the center of social gatherings.

Simone Schieler was raising her three children in the Hausgemeinschaft community. Paul, Willi, and Lilli looked up to MJ. In particular, elementary-aged Lilli enjoyed spending time with MJ. He was like a big brother who could make her

MJ and girlfriend Hannah van Bebber share a moment. PHOTO COURTESY VAN BEBBER FAMILY

laugh. He was kind and made her happy. He made her feel important. She had a crush on him as well. "He was an important part of my childhood because I saw him as the dream husband," Lilli said.

Many of those at Hausgemeinschaft were also central to the Bammental Mennonite Church, which has met for years in a borrowed room down the street. On Sunday mornings, twenty-five or thirty people gathered there to sing, read the Bible, and hear a sermon. The room and the crowd were small enough that no microphones were needed. A number of those attending were born Mennonite, either in Germany or the United States, but villagers who weren't Mennonite by heritage also attended. MJ preached a sermon there, in German, soon after he arrived in Bammental.

Though he was out of college and a bit older, he was part of the youth group at the church. The group played a lot of games together. The preferred contest was one called either "Mafia" or "Werewolf," in which people are assigned roles and the task is to figure out who has what role. Success in this game often requires convincing others to believe you, regardless of whether you are telling the truth. Not surprisingly, MJ was very good at it.

Shortly after he began spending time with the youth group, he began dating Hannah van Bebber, who was eighteen. She was taken by this cool American who could make others laugh. But aside from being funny, he was interesting and sensible. She saw how focused he could be and the range of topics that fascinated him for a time before he would get bored and move on.

MJ and Hannah fell in love. It was a simple, pure love that gave shape to his life and hers.

ℕ ℕ ℕ ℕ

Megan Rosenwink (née Rutt) could see multiple sides of MJ. She hadn't known him at EMU, since she graduated three years before him, but in Germany she was his supervisor as a volunteer for DMFK. For several months in the fall of 2006, she even shared a room at Hausgemeinschaft with him and another older woman. At times, conflict enters into that kind of common life as adults and sometimes children live together in tight quarters with some expectation of commonality and vulnerability. MJ defended Megan against the roommate when the woman acted unfairly toward her. He told Megan, "I understand if people don't get along with me, but everyone gets along with you."

He often told Megan about his sisters and other family members and his excitement for their accomplishments, which impressed her. Over time, she became another big sister to him. They talked together about their dating relationships and confided in each other.

Megan watched him in this stage between college and what came next, where he wasn't quite grown up, but wasn't a youth anymore. "My sense is he kind of got his stuff together," she said. "He definitely had this restlessness and slight dissatisfaction about how things were." She also watched him confront his depressive tendencies as he continued to dive into his work and relationships.

He could stand in the spotlight. He could make self-deprecating jokes. And he could be a dear friend who was not just present for but also engaged with the people with whom he shared time and space. "He was so authentic. I think that's what sticks with me," said Megan.

MJ and Megan went with friends to Oktoberfest together, and they traveled to Switzerland, where she snapped a photo of him on the shore of the Limmat River overlooking the spot where Anabaptist martyr Felix Manz was drowned for his faith.

As MJ was deep into his work counseling soldiers who had become disillusioned, he also discovered another way of relating to GIs and their commanding officers—through his poker skills. He showed Megan a notebook in which he was recording his winnings. His monthly stipend of 125 euros (about $160 USD at the time) wasn't much, though his room and board were covered. As he had in college, he played poker carefully and intentionally. "He was very diligent that he wasn't going to lose money," Megan said.

John once asked his son if he knew when to quit playing poker and whether he would lose money he didn't have.

MJ explained that he was always careful and rarely lost.

John asked, "Are you tithing your earnings?"

MJ grinned and said he'd think about it.

MJ won enough from soldiers, but not so much that he wasn't invited back to the games. "I know he padded his pockets here from soldiers from American bases," Megan said. While others would drink alcohol during the games, MJ would have one gin and tonic and then drink soda or tonic water without alcohol for the rest of the night. He was invited to games with military officers, and he told Simone, "I take their soldiers during the day and their money at night."

₪ ₪ ₪ ₪

In addition to working with soldiers and working on their possible cases, MJ and David gave presentations about their peacebuilding work with soldiers. David remembers going to Grenoble, France, to speak about their work at an academic conference. Their time was cut short, so they blitzed through their content with energy and enthusiasm. The auditorium erupted and the crowd gave them a standing ovation. At the end of the conference, the presenters gathered onstage and the moderator asked what motivated them. MJ said, "We're

Christians." There was an awkward pause, and the moderator moved on. Though David and MJ were often the only people identifying as Christian in the civic peace circles in which they worked, David marveled at the simplicity of the answer.

MJ had a deep respect for the faith and peace witness of his parents and grandparents, particularly John and his grandfather Mahlon. The reality of volunteering in a European country allowed MJ and David to reflect on and critique their faith and ideals. They were young Mennonites in a place between the church settings of their childhoods and the faith that they would forge for their adulthoods. They thrived in that in-between place, said David.

Their work was full of paradoxes, which only further sparked MJ's passion. From Sgt. Bob, they got unfiltered information and stories about the military that helped them connect with dozens of soldiers. They were young Mennonites becoming specialists on military hardware. MJ was playing poker with soldiers. And in their spare time, David and MJ would play the video game *Warcraft III* on networked computers, fighting orcs and trolls together.

The two young men worked alongside each other for nearly a year before David and his wife became youth pastors and he left the role with MCN in July 2006. Tim Huber came as a volunteer, and for three years he worked alongside MJ while also living at Hausgemeinschaft. As they continued the work together, Tim also found that MJ was adept at "discussing Tolstoy's writings on peace with Bavarian Communists, and then neatly pivoting to some guys with an 11 Bravo MOS and recounting the finer points of the Ma Deuce. That's a .50 caliber machine produced by Browning, something a lot of Mennonites wouldn't know."

MJ helped Tim learn both "military English" and German, which Tim didn't know as well. Occasionally, MJ would prank Tim by calling him on the MCN hotline and using a heavy

German accent. Tim would fumble around and eventually MJ would relent.

Together, Tim and MJ traveled to the United States in spring 2008 for eight weeks to speak on Mennonite college campuses and in high schools and churches.

On that trip, Robert Weiss accompanied the duo. He was an American soldier who had first called MCN having already read Mennonite writing on pacifism and just war theory.

The night before Robert's military trial in May 2008 in Vilseck, Germany, the trio of MJ, Robert, and Tim spent time talking about "theology, biblical translations, and church history —almost like every other evening we've ever spent together," wrote MJ in a Waterford Mennonite Church newsletter about his work with MCN.

Robert had pleaded guilty to charges of desertion and missing movement after he failed to report for duty. At the trial, he was shackled hand and foot. "This guy who refused to kill people and even turned himself in to military authorities was apparently too dangerous to be transferred out of the court room without restraints," MJ wrote. "At this point the irony of the whole situation was almost too much to take. Being willing to kill people, he was seen as society's 'protector.' Being unwilling to kill, he is seen as a danger to society. This 20-year-old kid, who one year before decided to read the New Testament for himself and come to his own conclusions, had gone from professional soldier to convicted criminal."

MJ expected Robert would get six to eight months in prison, and he was sentenced to seven.

Robert was one of the few people MJ counseled whose conscientious objector application was denied. The chances that an application would be approved were about fifty-fifty, but MJ's cases had an approval rate closer to 90 percent. MJ was devastated when applications were denied, and particularly after Robert's trial. He was invested in his appliers' success and competitive, if one can be, with an entire military and what it represented.

In one instance, MJ became a radical who helped a soldier escape. Agustín Aguayo had been trying to get out of the US Army since 2004. His application for conscientious objector status was denied twice. The first time he was in Iraq, he hadn't loaded his weapon on patrols. He filed his application in federal court when he got back from the Middle East and was denied three times. He told his chain of command he wasn't going back to Iraq and didn't pick up his weapon for a year, according to a blog post MJ wrote for the blog *Young Anabaptist Radicals*. Agustín was ordered to ship out on the night of December 1, 2006. "So, Agustin made himself 'unavailable' during the final deployment formation (aka he went for a drive at an undisclosed location)," MJ wrote.

The next morning, Agustín turned himself in at the military police station.

They all expected that Agustín would be court-martialed, given an honorable discharge, and put in jail for five to nine months. Instead, he was taken home and told to get his gear to ship out. The company commander told them, "He's going to Iraq, even if we have to handcuff him and force him on the plane."

MJ wrote that Agustín made the choice to jump out the bedroom window, run out the front gate of the base, and "disappear into the German afternoon sunlight."

The military police were waiting and frantically began searching for him when they realized what had happened. They didn't find his hiding spot. MJ wrote passionately on *Young Anabaptist Radicals* about what that meant:

> It was one of those situations that I've read about, but it seemed quite different when I was involved. War resistance has been an

issue that Anabaptists have dealt with for hundreds of years. Since the founding of the United States, "peace churches" have struggled with how to respond to the forced military service. We have great stories of our ancestors refusing to fight during the Civil War, struggling to be recognized as conscientious objectors during World War I and World War II, and refusing the draft during Vietnam. But today there is no draft; there is no forced conscription, just an all-volunteer military. In many ways, it was the end of our interaction with the military. We stand outside the bases occasionally and express our opposition in the form of a pithy phrase or two, but our country's wars no longer require any sacrifice or struggle on our part. At the start of the current war in Iraq, we were told to go on with our lives as before. I specifically remember being told to "keep shopping." And so we do.

People like Agustin Aguayo are a reminder that there is a war going on, with real people fighting, dying, and being changed by their experiences. The front line of conscientious objection is no longer in our churches or in the courts. The front line of conscientious objection is within the professional military. I hope that we, as life-long conscientious objectors who no longer have the big personal investment in our nation's wars, can remain active in the struggle, by supporting those who come to their beliefs through their wartime experiences. It's one way we can actively respond to the wars we are funding. Agustin needs our help, and we can provide him and others like him with something other than bullets for their M-16s.[2]

In March 2007, Agustín was convicted of desertion in Wurzburg, Germany, and sentenced to eight months in prison. Amnesty International named him a prisoner of conscience as he was released from the military. He was awarded the Stuttgart Peace Prize in December 2007.

ℶ ℶ ℶ ℶ

During those years in Bammental, MJ also traveled to do non-violent peacemaking work in hot spots, including both Iraq and Afghanistan in 2007 and Israel/Palestine in 2009. Even a risk-taker like Sgt. Bob questioned his decision to go on such trips.

In July 2007, MJ flew to Kabul at a time when kidnappings were on the rise.

"The problem with this is that my relatives were informed that central Afghanistan is relatively safe, and this news will definitely worry them. And that's really the biggest drawback to the entire trip—I don't want people to be constantly worried," he wrote in his journal.

After two kidnapped Germans were later found dead, he added, "The deaths will be hugely publicized in Germany, and I hate to think how much more Hannah and Hausgemeinschaft might worry. It's silly for me to worry about them worrying, but I don't want my actions causing anyone pain."

In November, he went to Iraq for ten days as part of a delegation that included two men from Lancaster, Pennsylvania. On the second day of the trip, MJ learned that the duo's priorities were not the medical and psychological help the group was there to offer "but rather spiritual warfare," he wrote in a trip journal. The men were on a mission to "cleanse the land by praying away Muslim spirits at holy sites," according to John Sharp.

MJ referred to the trip as a "twilight zone." Later he would tell friends and family of how scared he was on that trip.

One evening, MJ spent two hours at dinner talking to a Kurdish military leader who he later learned had led successful campaigns against Saddam Hussein for twenty years. The following day, the group met with one of the most powerful women in Kurdistan, who had worked to protect women from legal killings and to require a married woman's approval before her husband could take another wife.

MJ was elated at the connections he made and how "doors flew open" as a result. In addition to the conversations and unexpected experiences, MJ attended lectures on mental health and visited two prisons and an orphanage. The trip piqued his interest in the country as well as in psychology and counseling. On that trip, MJ learned about post-traumatic stress disorder, something he would later suffer himself because of his peace-making work.

After he returned to Germany, he wrote that he had little hope for peace on the national level in the next decade or even in his lifetime. "It would be easy to give up on the idea of waging peace—very easy in fact," he wrote.

Yet on the individual level, MJ was deeply hopeful. In his journal, MJ referenced Robert Young Pelton, who wrote that the truly interesting and educational things on the planet occur in areas of high intensity, often war zones. MJ wrote, "I would add to that by saying that these conflict zones are also hot zones for high-intensity work of the spirit. And it is this that continues to inspire me and give me hope."

₪ ₪ ₪ ₪

In the fall of 2008, as MJ's three-year term with Military Counseling Network and DMFK was coming to an end, he joked that he was going to become an emergency medical technician or a "sandwich artist." Early in his time in Bammental, he'd joked that he wanted to become president of the United States someday, and someone playfully inserted his name into the design used by Barack Obama's 2008 presidential campaign.

He applied for a master's degree program at Philipps-Universität Marburg and was accepted to work toward a degree in peace studies and conflict resolution. He moved from Hausgemeinschaft and Bammental about a hundred miles north to begin his studies.

Returning to academia seemed to drag MJ down. On weekends he would travel from Marburg to Bammental via train— riding for free, eating as much as he wanted in Bammental, and taking food back with him. Hiltrude Krauss, Wolfgang's spouse and one of the originators of Hausgemeinschaft, mothered him and offered him as much as she could. Megan sent him back with her homemade granola, not telling him about how many carbs or how much sugar it had. "MJ had a lot of mothers and sisters around the world," Megan said.

Hannah joined him in Marburg, living with him in an apartment. He was focused on his studies and sometimes annoyed by them.

Life was somehow more intense for him and Hannah than it had been in Bammental, she said. He was taking antidepressants, but she often saw him struggle to get out of bed and engage others as he had before. She urged him to seek therapy, though he didn't at that point.

He often told her, "I need to do something useful," so he continued to try to find those activities. As he had told friends and family at the time, he was sometimes poor at leading a well-balanced life.

As he worked on the thesis required for his degree, he used a new software called MAXQDA to do qualitative research of blogs from Israeli settlers in the West Bank. The thesis work combined his love for technology and his writing ability. He used the software to assess how often different bloggers used a word. From there, he could analyze the narrative, which he valued more than the data. "Narratives can answer the 'who' questions: Who am I? Who are we? Where did I/we come from? Who are those other people?" he wrote in his thesis.

His research also highlighted the importance of narratives in framing what has happened, how things work now, and what may happen in the future. Narratives can help people understand morality, how decisions were made, and how those come together in a culture. "Understanding the cultural master narratives, then, individuals and small groups have the option of reframing their actions within a different narrative, a competing narrative," he wrote in his thesis. "While they are never completely incompatible with the master narratives, they tweak them in a way so that their actions make sense, and they may even be considered heroic."

He had first encountered the Israeli/Palestinian conflict on a 2009 trip as an intern with Christian Peacemaker Teams. Now as an academic, he could articulate that understanding the narrative can help one approach the conflict with a broader context and more nuance and thus suggest different possible solutions. "For those seeking to encourage positive change in the Israel-Palestine conflict, and especially those who have recognized the ideological settlers as a critical conflict party, the importance of their narrative cannot be ignored or cast as irrelevant or mad," he wrote.

With that dissertation, MJ earned his master's degree and prepared to return to the United States. He was ready to have a job to earn more money and to be closer to family, particularly his beloved grandfather Mahlon, whose health was faltering.

The Bible leaves no doubt at all about the sanctity of the act of worldmaking, or of the world that was made, or of creaturely or bodily life in this world. We are holy creatures living among other holy creatures in a world that is holy. Some people know this, and some do not. Nobody, of course, knows it all the time. But what keeps it from being far better known than it is? Why is it apparently unknown to millions of professed students of the Bible? How can modern Christianity have so solemnly folded its hands while so much of the work of God was and is being destroyed?

—**WENDELL BERRY**, *The Art of the Commonplace*

SEVEN

Into the Heart of Africa

WHEN MJ RETURNED to Indiana in 2010, he became a salesman once again.

The president of the company that made MAXQDA, the qualitative analysis software package MJ had used in graduate school for his thesis, hired him to be its first salesperson in the United States. He printed business cards and rented an office in downtown Goshen at the corner of Main and Washington in a building called the Famous.

MJ had big hopes as he returned to the Midwest. After being in voluntary service and then graduate school overseas, he hoped to make money to help his family pay off debts. He also hoped to be part of a growing enterprise. And he looked forward to being near his grandparents, particularly as Mahlon's health was growing more fragile.

He and Hannah were also at a tender stage of their relationship. They had deep and abiding love for each other, but the time in Marburg had been difficult. As MJ dreamed of going to dangerous places in the world and left Germany, they were on the path toward breaking up. They remained friends and in communication, yet it was difficult for both of them.

MJ lived most of 2010 and the start of 2011 on Seventh Street in Goshen in a house owned by childhood friend Keith Grubaugh and his wife Jenna. When the couple went to the Philippines for three years with Mennonite Central Committee, they rented out the house to friends, eventually including MJ.

MJ did seminars on MAXQDA and went to trade shows. He spent time with his grandparents. He dated. He renewed a connection with Justin Ramer, a former Bethany classmate who was living and working in Goshen. They played darts together at Constant Spring, the first bar in Goshen owned and operated by a Mennonite. Justin, known by his last name Ramer, had like MJ lost his baby face in the years since high school. As they played darts, they bantered and taunted one another. Ramer was the better player and usually won, but on the rare occasion when MJ came out on top, he would dance and crow about the accomplishment.

Yet those moments of joy became more rare for MJ in that year. He missed the energy he got from the work he'd done in Germany, and he missed Hannah, the woman he had grown to love. Trying to sell MAXQDA was making him miserable. He loved showing others how to use the software, but was tired of the pressure to sell and no longer wanted to do that, according to his father.

While his housemates were extroverted and social, MJ grew more introverted and slept more as he battled depression. He had less energy. His world was getting smaller. When Keith and Jenna returned from the Philippines, Keith found his best friend "shriveling up." The MJ who was usually vibrant and full of life wasn't the one he now saw.

That time in Goshen helped teach MJ about what he really wanted. He wasn't ready to settle into the life that involved doing conventional work in one of the places where other lifetime Mennonites had gathered. He realized that following passion and doing work about which he was enthusiastic was more important to him than money or image. "The life that would have kept him alive and safe wouldn't have kept him happy at the time," said Keith.

ℕ ℕ ℕ ℕ

Suzanne and Tim Lind were looking for someone special.

The Linds were veterans of overseas relief and peacemaking work. From 1968 to 1970, they were both students in the country that was then called Zaire, and Tim was in alternative service because of the draft for the Vietnam War. After they married, they were in the African countries of Madagascar and South Africa with several different church agencies. By 2011, they were country representatives for Mennonite Central Committee in the Democratic Republic of the Congo. Much of their work was in Kinshasa, in the western part of the country.

They needed someone to work in the eastern part of the country, where refugees crowded into camps and armed groups continued to battle. They wanted someone who could teach nonviolent methods of peacemaking and distribute resources to those who were in the United Nations camps for internally displaced persons (IDPs). They first reached out to Sarah Nahar (née Thompson), who had been at Bethany Christian with MJ and was finishing her master of divinity degree at Associated Mennonite Biblical Seminary in Elkhart. She wasn't interested in the job, but thought of MJ and suggested his name. "I knew he wouldn't only not be freaked out by it, but thrive in that spot," said Sarah.

Soon MJ and Suzanne met at a Goshen coffee shop, to discuss the assignment. MJ had already started research before that October morning and asked good questions. Suzanne was a bit intimidated by his intelligence, charm, and wit. "I was just so taken aback by his confidence mixed with humor," she said. "I liked him immediately."

In addition to someone who could handle the rigor of the relief and peacemaking work, they needed someone who could speak French well. Though more than two hundred languages are spoken in the country, French remains the official and dominant language in the wake of the colonial rule of Belgium.

MJ hadn't studied French. He hadn't worked in Africa. The only African stamp in his passport was from South Africa, when he went with Sgt. Bob and his family on what was more of a vacation than anything else. Germany and the DRC are essentially polar opposites. Modern-day Germany is orderly, powerful, and democratic. The DRC is chaotic and raw and run dictatorially.

Yet MJ loved languages and relished a reason to learn a new one. He offered to use Rosetta Stone software and a tutor to learn French in the months before leaving Goshen for the DRC. He asked for a reading list from Suzanne and Tim to learn more about the country. And he asked for community.

He knew from his time in Marburg and Goshen that he needed not only meaningful work, but also people around him who would provide support. Suzanne told Tim, "Michael is a team player, a person who thrives on interaction, lively discussion of ideas and plans, and a strong friendship base. We will want to think carefully about how support for friendship, mentoring, working group, nurture could be attended to appropriately if Michael would be placed in eastern Congo."

MJ was offered and accepted the position. He finished his commitments to MAXQDA and headed for Akron,

Pennsylvania, in July 2012. After orientation with the other new MCC volunteers and staff in Akron, MJ headed to Brussels, Belgium. It put another stamp in his passport, and placed him in French classes in the very city from which King Leopold had ruled the land where MJ was headed next.

ּ ּ ּ ּ

In the latter half of the 1800s, a series of characters circled Congo like animals eyeing prey.

British doctor David Livingstone had started exploring Africa in the 1840s. He had found Victoria Falls and searched for the source of the Nile. He was the first white man to cross the continent from coast to coast, though two biracial slave traders made the round trip first. When he hadn't returned to England for years, journalist Henry Morton Stanley went looking for him. Stanley did indeed find him, and his recounting of their meeting, in which he uttered the now famous words "Dr. Livingstone, I presume" in November 1871, made him a rich travel writer.

In Brussels, King Leopold II followed the news. He was thirty-seven at the time and hadn't grown out of the awkwardness of his youth or the need for his father's approval. He watched the English and Spanish reaping the rewards of colonization and wanted the same for Belgium. He told one of his advisors, "Belgium doesn't exploit the world. It's a taste we have got to make her learn."[1]

He had ascended the throne in 1865 and wanted to do more than build lavishly in his own country. Stanley had continued to explore the African continent, including fifteen hundred miles of the Congo River, and Leopold wanted to meet him, which finally happened in 1878. Stanley agreed to set up a base near the mouth of the Congo River and became "Leopold's man in the Congo," according to journalist and historian Adam Hochschild in his book *King Leopold's Ghost*.[2]

Stanley got the Indigenous chiefs to sign their land over to Leopold, essentially stealing it in the typical way of colonizers. Stanley's bestselling book *The Congo and the Founding of Its Free State: A Story of Work and Exploration*, edited by Leopold, referred to the new colony as the International Association of the Congo.[3] Leopold went abroad to seek recognition of his colony and established himself as King-Sovereign of the Congo Free State in 1885. Within a few years, he established the Force Publique as his army to ensure order and obedience and the flow of ivory to outposts along the river so that it could be shipped to Europe.

However, the rubber boom is what defined Leopold's grip on the Congo. By the early 1890s, people wanted rubber for tires, hoses, tubing, and more. The boom was on. Congo was rich with wild vines that released rubber sap when sliced or cut, and Leopold demanded it from the country he was now running like a militarized corporation.

His enforcers often cut off the hands of the Congolese who didn't deliver enough rubber. As men in search of fortune or just a place to satisfy their cruel thirst for blood found opportunity in Leopold's Congo Free State, the value of a human life was low. The Congolese people—men, women, and children—were seen as nothing more than labor. Hochschild writes that because Leopold's state wasn't trying to eliminate an ethnic group, it wasn't technically a genocide—though the number of deaths resulted in some calling it that.[4] Murder and massacres were common. Soldiers burned villages, hunted the people who had lived in them, and either killed or captured them. Starvation and disease killed many more.

Belgian estimates of the population in Congo indicated that it was cut "by at least half" between 1880 and 1920. Counts confirmed around ten million people living there in the 1920s, meaning approximately ten million people had died over the course of thirty years.

Calls for reform in the Congo finally led Leopold to sell the territory to the Belgian government in 1908, a year before his death. One estimate is that as the only colonizer to singularly own a country, he had made $1.1 billion in today's dollars.

נ נ נ נ

Leaving behind the life he knew in Europe and the United States, MJ arrived in the Democratic Republic of the Congo in August 2012. He didn't come to conquer, as had the white explorers of old. He came to aid and assist, to learn and listen.

He was part of a team of eleven MCCers in the Rwanda/ Burundi region, but he was a thousand miles from the nearest MCCer in the Congo. The massive country is nearly double the size of Western Europe and over one-fourth the size of the overall area of the United States. Since the 1960s, the country's infrastructure has not been maintained, and no highways run from Kinshasa, the capital in the west, to the eastern side of Congo. The DRC doesn't have many paved roads, something MJ would often joke about, and something that other expatriates, or expats as they're called, often note when they're talking about travel.

He survived his first infection or parasite with a few days in bed and antibiotics. Yet, emotionally, he was healthier than he'd been in years as he faced a new challenge.

One of the first things he did after arriving in the Congo was buy a motorcycle. He got a small cycle with a 125 cc engine manufactured in China that he could ride for hours on almost any terrain. While some expats demanded to move about in Land Cruisers or with escorts, MJ avoided that mindset. He preferred to ride.

MJ settled in Bukavu, on the southern end of Lake Kivu. He found an apartment that was part of a compound with four residences and hired staff members, including gardeners, night watchmen, and at times a house cleaner for the residences. One of the reasons MJ picked the spot was because he hoped to raise his own food. The owner approved of his planting a garden and building hutches for animals, including chickens, guinea pigs, and rabbits. The question was whether it would go better than his attempt at worm farming in the college dorm.

Part of his job with MCC was to be a point person for agricultural training in eastern Congo, yet the larger focus was on peacemaking and working with internally displaced people.

In an MCC publication, he described his assignment this way: "As coordinator for MCC's work in the eastern Democratic Republic of the Congo, I support the Congolese Protestant Council of Churches and its agencies that work in emergency response and for peace and reconciliation in the region. Their projects respond to the needs of displaced people, support victims of violence and encourage armed groups to demobilize and reintegrate into society."[5]

About a third of the time, he worked in Bukavu from his home and an office there. The rest of the time he traveled in the North Kivu and South Kivu provinces to visit partners, projects, and IDP camps. He often worked with Emmanuel Billay or Moise Butimbushi, who trained him as a colleague in the Program of Peace and Reconciliation (PPR). That program with the Protestant Council of Churches sprouted from a response to the Rwandan genocide of 1994 and the two subsequent civil wars.

The three men often traveled together, walking for miles. MJ carried a walking stick and traveled with both an open mind and a willingness to engage rather than expect special treatment.

Some expats ask for special food, or sometimes those hosting them make what they think an expat would want: milk, bread, sugar, and french fries with mayonnaise.

MJ is exhausted from traveling the rough roads of the DRC by motorcycle.
PHOTO USED BY PERMISSION OF MENNONITE CENTRAL COMMITTEE

MJ would give such offerings to others and instead eat what the locals were eating: fish and fufu, a daily staple made with cassava flour or corn flour. He was also fond of sombe, made from boiled and pounded cassava leaves.

If Emmanuel and Moise had to sleep on the ground, so would MJ.

If they were hot and sweaty as they walked and they came to a river, the men would swim together, MJ assuring them that doing so wouldn't get them in trouble with their bosses.

He would wear the same clothes for days on end if needed.

As his French skills improved, he also worked at learning Swahili, which was spoken among some in eastern Congo. He was embarrassed at times that his Swahili wasn't perfect, yet he would ask Emmanuel and Moise for words that were important to a particular village as they approached it to do their work. MJ's small efforts at language went a long way in gaining trust and building relationships with those he encountered. "When you go into the village and the white person greets you, it just makes you happy," said Moise.

MJ was a white North American, so it was unexpected that he would willingly choose to forgo the comforts of home. Yet he insisted, and that humility impressed the Congolese and earned their respect. He wasn't like the other white people the Congolese had known.

"He was very open. And totally engaged in his work. He was kind, showed affection and love. He listened very well and a lot. He wanted to know the truth," said Emmanuel, adding that MJ wanted to feel the truth, not just know it.

MJ didn't go to the DRC to evangelize, as had so many white people before him. Rather, Mennonite Central Committee works with and supports the three denominations of Congolese Mennonites, in addition to some Mennonite Brethren in the country. Those churches operate programs to help internally displaced people. And some of those national churches then evangelize, sharing the gospel and trying to get people to repent and give their heart to Christ, said Mulanda "Jimmy" Juma, the peacebuilding coordinator for MCC in southern Africa. But MCC itself doesn't engage in evangelism. "MCC doesn't allow that," he said. "It's not an opportunity to preach."

MJ showed love for others and modeled the life of Christ. His actions demonstrated his faith via love, compassion, and trust. Some of the Congolese Mennonite groups also saw their numbers grow because of their relief work. "The evangelization was not done through preaching. It was done through action," said Jimmy.

In an MCC publication in the fall of 2013, MJ put his work into context: "Places of intense conflict are also places where creative solutions are born and put to the test. If Jesus' example is for everyone everywhere, what does that look like in eastern Congo, where war has been the norm for 20 years? I get to work on the front line of Congolese ingenuity and faithfulness in response to violence and hardship."[6]

ℝ ℝ ℝ ℝ

When MJ arrived in the DRC, he helped coordinate a program offering food, seeds, and supplies to internally displaced persons and others in North and South Kivu.

The Canadian Foodgrains Bank, which MCC created in the early 1980s to work toward ending global hunger, had grown to become a partnership of fifteen major Christian churches and church-based agencies in Canada to offer food aid in emergencies and engage in longer-term advocacy for food security. The growing number of displaced people in the DRC provinces meant that the Church of Christ in the Congo Ministry for Refugees and Emergencies, known by the French acronym ECC-MERU, was overwhelmed. The combat between the rebel group M23 and the Congolese army Forces armées de la république démocratique du Congo (FARDC) was forcing thousands of families to flee their homes, and with few belongings. MJ helped with the administration to keep funding and supplies flowing in the right directions to help those people.

MJ attended nearly weekly meetings with ECC-MERU on its work and developed relationships with those who worked in the programs he helped administer. How they were able to move food, tarps, hoes, and seeds depended on so many factors, including budgets and reports, as well as how people were on the move in response to fighting among armed groups. MJ learned and adapted quickly. When Suzanne Lind visited him in late 2012, she reported back that she was "very, very happy that he is getting so well established in such a solid way." She was impressed with his French and his "calm and careful reactions to the insecurity in Goma."

"Everyone with whom I spoke had positive, thankful things to say about Michael," she wrote in a report.

MCC and ECC-MERU had established a plan to spend nearly $300,000 on food aid to help feed twelve thousand people in two towns in North and South Kivu that had thousands of displaced persons. This included a group of southern villages accessible only on foot that had become a haven for armed groups as a result. In both areas, the residents historically raised livestock on the fertile land. But the conflict since the civil wars had resulted in a massive decline in livestock production on the small farms and therefore a huge increase in food insecurity. Along with Somalia, the DRC had the lowest food security in the world at the time.

Cassava, potatoes, corn, beans, and soybeans could all be grown year-round, with two planting and harvest seasons. But from September to November, as families awaited harvest, they relied on food aid.

Families who had little themselves took in family members or neighbors who were displaced, adding to the stress and need for food. Sometimes these host families even took in strangers. One woman told MJ she did so because she had been displaced in the past.

As he traveled, MJ asked people who were displaced and the ones who were hosting them in villages how many meals a day they were eating. Most of them were eating only one meal a day, and the host families had no seeds to plant.

MCC reports described the crisis this way:

The latest outbreak of fighting began in April 2012, when Congolese army officers mutinied and rallied a dissident force that has since engaged the Congolese army and attacked civilian villages. . . . Officers were soon joined by additional defectors from the Congolese army, members of local militia groups, and conscripted civilians. . . .

In the process about 470,000 newly displaced people have abandoned their villages due to the fighting. Most of these are in North Kivu, but many have spilled over into South Kivu, as well as Rwanda and Uganda. The latest crisis has pushed the total number of displaced in Congo to more than 2,000,000 for the first time since 2009. About ¾ of this total are in North and South Kivu.[7]

As of 2019, the DRC had more internally displaced people than every other country in the world except Syria. The Rwandan genocide and two subsequent civil wars in the Congo resulted in millions of displaced people in Africa's second largest country. In 2013, there were about 3 million internally displaced persons, and another 1 million or so were displaced that year. That number grew to more than 5.5 million by 2020.

The partners of MCC and ECC-MERU worked in IDP camps in both North and South Kivu and areas where armed groups pillaged fields and livestock. The agencies sometimes distributed tarps to several hundred families to replace the banana leaves that they were using on their shelters during the rainy season, when children were particularly vulnerable to illness.

After the 2012 outburst of violence, MJ worked with ECC-MERU to create a project plan in 2013 and 2014 that acknowledged that it couldn't address the fundamental causes of food insecurity, but it could create some infrastructure to procure and distribute 150 tons of cornmeal, 60 tons of beans, 9,000 liters of vegetable oil, 3 tons of salt, 15 tons of bean seeds, 10 tons of corn seeds, and 2,000 hoes.

For the most part, the project worked.

Over several years, two thousand families each received 75 kilograms of corn meal, 30 kilograms of beans, 1.5 kilograms of salt, and 5 liters of vegetable oil, plus a hoe and seeds. Recipients didn't always follow the agricultural training or even successfully raise a crop, but they ate more and ate better over time. MCC and ECC-MERU started similar projects in other camps often overlooked by other aid organizations.

Distributions didn't always go smoothly, which frustrated MJ. Families were to present a piece of paper noting that they were eligible to receive items and would sign their names or use a thumbprint to indicate that they had received them, but people who didn't have paperwork wanted to be added to the list. Trucks broke down or got stuck in the mud. Violence from rebel groups or government soldiers would force a planned event to be canceled. MJ grew most frustrated with people working in the ECC-MERU programs. When planning and implementation didn't go as he hoped, he stepped in, though he would often feel guilty that he was doing so. "When I first arrived in Congo, I saw other expats absolutely screaming at Congolese coworkers and later explaining that this was the only way to get anything done," he wrote. "I remember thinking that if I ever came to such a point, I would need to leave immediately. Even the fact that I totally took control of the distribution that was getting out of control is a bad sign. That's not what I'm supposed to be doing."[8]

₪ ₪ ₪ ₪

MJ regularly traveled to meet with leaders of armed groups in North and South Kivu.

These weren't highly formal meetings. As NPR reporter Greg Warner described it, "Not far from the lake were rebel-held forests, where every few weeks Sharp would walk, unarmed, to the base of a particularly fearsome rebel group called the FDLR. And there he would sit in the shade of banana trees to drink tea, practice his Swahili, and listen to these rebel stories."[9]

The original audio from the story, first aired in January 2015, quotes MJ talking about building relationships and trust to bring about peace. "You can always listen," MJ told Warner. "You can always listen to people who want a chance to talk about how they see the world."

A few months after arriving in the DRC, MJ had walked with three others for two hours to meet with an FDLR leader. The lieutenant colonel told MJ that they didn't want to overthrow the Rwandan government by force. "This would 'just continue the cycle of violence,'" MJ reported him saying. Yet Rwandan officials in Kigali didn't want to talk to the FDLR, the man said. President Paul Kagame needed to be pressured to talk to them.

Serge Lungele and Bishop Bulambo Lembelcmbe Josué of the Peace and Reconciliation Program remember the meeting.

"Have you ever met an FDLR before?" the colonel asked.

"No," MJ said. "This is the first time."

"What do you see? Are they human beings or are they animals?"

"I see they are human beings, as we are."

The officer favored repatriation but said that some of the other officers didn't. He saw value in letting some go home, including the sick, women whose husbands had been killed in fighting, or those who no longer wanted to fight.

MJ asked the man why he was willing to work with them and let people leave and go back to Rwanda. The lieutenant colonel said that 90 percent of the current FDLR fighters were less than ten years old in 1994 when the genocide occurred. He said the genocidaires should be tried in an international criminal court, including those in the current regime in Kigali. "We're tired. We're ready to go home," the man said.

MJ listened. He wore a white polo shirt with a blue collar bearing the ECC logo. That shirt identifying him as a church worker did offer him some protection in these settings. In his trip report, MJ included a photo of himself with four armed FDLR fighters. The lieutenant colonel urged MJ to be their spokesperson in the world, to tell people what was really happening. "Michael, we are human beings. Don't think we're animals," he said.

Moise Butimbushi and Emmanuel Billay, field officers with PPR, would make arrangements for them to travel to meet with rebels. Visitors can't just walk into militia camps. You have to ask if you can come and be received.

On one trip, a militia leader told MJ that white people bring wars to the Congo. Rwanda had invaded DRC and killed people, but no one had come to help, the leader said.

MJ was calm. He asked for permission to talk.

He asked the leader if he had really killed twenty-five officers.

He explained that he was there to demobilize combatants. He explained that fewer people arming themselves and using violence to solve a problem would help everyone.

MJ had connected with the militia leader, whom some would call a warlord. MJ had spent five days in the same pants and shirt so that he could travel to meet someone who was both a perpetrator and a victim of the violence. Moise was worried that he hadn't provided soap and a proper bed for MJ, but MJ didn't care. He was looking for something other than comfort and separation.

"Every place we went with Michael, he was always finding a way to connect with those warlords," said Moise.

MJ would listen to the rebels, sometimes as they told of the magic gris-gris they believed protected them from bullets.

MJ also challenged them. In one meeting, MJ pointed out that the militia was burning and doing damage in the region. "So you're using violence against violence," MJ told the leader.

The chief with whom he was meeting said he couldn't control everyone and that there had been miscommunication, that he needed to talk to the other side to make peace. MJ said he needed agreement from the leader to go to the other side and help work for peace. The leader agreed to participate in a process as long as the government wasn't part of it and MJ wouldn't side with the enemy.

"The church is neutral," said MJ.

MJ didn't realize that the man was the head of Raia Mutomboki, a violent rebel group. "He looked like a jovial old grandpa next door that would give you some tips on how to better fertilize your lawn," MJ wrote.[10] Their motorcycle drivers were alarmed that MJ had met with him.

The trips were sometimes challenging, particularly in terms of the travel itself. They rode motorcycles over the dirty, rutted roads, and Emmanuel told MJ that he shouldn't talk at roadblocks. MJ shrugged and said he had been in Afghanistan and this wasn't a big deal. Yet people were surprised to see the *mzungu*—the Swahili word for a white person—on a motorcycle.

When they encountered roadblocks, MJ would ignore the armed men who stopped them and would pretend he didn't understand what anyone was saying. Emmanuel would

MJ meets with Mwami Elenge Mwemano (*left*), head of the armed group Raia Mutomboki, accompanied by Emmanuel Billay. PHOTO USED BY PERMISSION OF MENNONITE CENTRAL COMMITTEE

negotiate with them, paying far less than if MJ had done so as a mzungu.

ַ ₪ ₪ ₪

Amid the hard, heavy work, MJ soaked in the beauty of the Congo.

Amid the beauty of eastern DRC is a national park that brings pride to the Congolese and a safe haven for a third of the world's endangered wild mountain gorillas. Virunga National Park is a UNESCO World Heritage Site guarded by armed rangers who protect the gorillas and other wildlife that inhabit its three thousand plus square miles. It's a popular destination for tourists and expats who can make their way near the border with Rwanda and Uganda.

With Serge Lungele, one of his coworkers with PPR, MJ visited Virunga and was returning to Goma when they saw a soldier who wanted their Land Cruiser to stop. They were wary and kept going. After traveling another mile, they encountered a bus that was blocking the road. Serge was terrified. He remembers MJ telling him not to be afraid.

MJ got out of the vehicle and started talking to the group of armed men who were surrounding the bus and standing over the passengers, who had been forced to exit the bus and lie facedown on the ground. The bandits were robbing them, and the soldier down the road had been trying to keep Serge and MJ's vehicle from coming across the robbery in progress.

MJ started talking to the bandits in French. He asked them what they were doing. "How are you doing this to people in your own country?" he asked.

The bandits fled into the bush. The bus driver, who had also run and hid, was persuaded to come out of hiding. MJ and Serge stayed until the passengers reboarded the bus and were on their way down the road again.

MJ was from another country. He didn't have to be in the Congo, much less put himself in danger on behalf of the Congolese. Yet as he encountered a violent situation, he stopped, walked up, and engaged in conversation. He challenged men holding guns to rethink what they were doing to their countrypeople. He couldn't fix all the problems in the country and prevent all the violence. Yet in this situation, he could do something and he did.

"As a Congolese, that was a lesson to me," said Serge.

Was it wise for MJ to confront armed bandits? On that day, his peacemaking effort worked. Yet this was, and still is, a dangerous area. In 2021, Luca Attanasio, the Italian ambassador to the DRC, was killed along with two others in an apparent kidnapping attempt near Virunga National Park as they traveled to visit a UN World Food Program site. Occasionally, violent incidents, including attacks on the park rangers, make international news. But what MJ did that day wasn't heralded in news reports. It was just something he did.

In the vehicle, as they drove on, MJ told Serge, "If you are with me and we come into such situations, don't be afraid."

He told Serge there were two reasons why he didn't have fear in those situations.

The first was, "If they take us into the bush with them, my country, which is the US, will come and look for me."

The second was, "If they kill us, which can also happen, no problem. Our blood can change things in your country."

History lies heavy on Africa: the long decades of colonialism, several hundred years of the Atlantic and Arab world slave trade, and—all too often ignored—countless centuries of indigenous slavery before that. From the colonial era, the major legacy Europe left to Africa was not democracy as it is practiced today in countries like England, France, and Belgium; it was authoritarian rule and plunder. On the whole continent, perhaps no nation has had a harder time than the Congo in emerging from the shadow of its past.

—ADAM HOCHSCHILD, *King Leopold's Ghost*

EIGHT

Peace Not Plunder

THE STORY OF CENTRAL AFRICA over the past five hundred years is one where greed and hope, suffering and resilience, flow together like the waters of the Congo River, the massive strand that stretches 2,715 miles.

What others in the world know of the Democratic Republic of the Congo often doesn't take in the range of loss and riches that is part of that history. If an American high school student can name something about the land that is now the DRC, it likely comes from *Heart of Darkness*, the novel by Joseph Conrad first published in 1899. Conrad had traveled to the Congo in 1890 and was horrified by what he saw. His novel exposes how horribly people can treat one another, particularly within the construct of colonialism.

The book that is now more than a century old has probably done more to shape the popular view of the region than any other single work. And its critique of colonialism continues to shape our understanding of the past. "The conquest of the earth, which mostly means taking it away from those who have a different complexion or slightly flatter nose than ourselves, is not a pretty thing when you look into it too much," Conrad wrote.[1]

In the final section of *Heart of Darkness*, the central character Kurtz utters, "The horror! The horror!" The novel's explorations of both the depth of sin in human nature and the horrific impact of colonialism remain powerful lessons even as the book's readers do well to recognize that its portrayals of Africans and women are fraught with deep racism and sexism. In *King Leopold's Ghost*, Adam Hochschild writes, "However laden it is with Victorian racism, *Heart of Darkness* remains the greatest portrait in fiction of Europeans in the Scramble for Africa."[2]

It is difficult to absorb and make sense of all the horrors Congo has experienced, and why, over the past five hundred years. Congolese researcher and activist Fidel Bafilemba and American human rights activist John Prendergast frame the waves of conquest in their book, *Congo Stories: Battling Five Centuries of Exploitation and Greed.*[3]

First, the New World needed labor on plantations. An estimated four million people were put on ships along the 250-mile shore of the Congo, destined for enslavement in the Americas. (One in four people enslaved on plantations in the American South came from equatorial Africa, according to historians.)[4]

Then the need for ivory and rubber for tires on the growing number of automobiles led to Leopold II running Congo as his own private corporation.

The need for copper for World War I weapons motivated the West to raid Congo's bountiful supply.

In World War II, America bested Nazi Germany in the race to control Congo's uranium as the United States developed a nuclear weapon.

Competition for metals and minerals during the Cold War between the United States and Soviet Union led the United

States and Belgium to assassinate Patrice Lumumba, the newly elected prime minister, and support a coup that installed a dictator who raided the country for his own wealth rather than the good of the people.

Then others came for the diamonds. And others have returned to take more of the metals and minerals. Beneath the soil of the DRC is one of the richest collections of wealth, a veritable periodic table to feed our growing reliance on technology.[5]

₪ ₪ ₪ ₪

Anton Jongeneel, a member of the US Foreign Service, had been in central Africa only a short time on that day in 2013 when he sat poolside at the fancy Serena Hotel in Gisenyi, Rwanda. Anton's predecessor had passed along a list of potential new contacts. MJ's name was on that list. "Nobody knew who Michael Sharp was back then," Anton said.

Anton sent a note to MJ saying he would be in Gisenyi. MJ arrived on time and said he had ridden six hours on a motorcycle for the meeting. He was dirty and disheveled as he showed up, and Anton felt bad for him.

"I wasn't sure I wanted the meeting. But because he had ridden six hours, I gave him the time," Anton said.

MJ asked for a glass of water, but upon seeing the ice in the glass of gin and tonic added, "I think I'll have one of those too."

As he had done so many times with others, MJ impressed and charmed Anton, who quickly realized MJ knew things others didn't. He was meeting with rebel leaders who had been involved in the Rwandan genocide. He understood the FDLR and how it operated. Anton was intrigued; he had never heard of Mennonite Central Committee or the programs with which MJ was working.

Anton had been a federal prosecutor in Washington, D.C., and did a stint at the International Criminal Tribunal for

Rwanda in Tanzania. That made him interested in eastern Congo, and he got a posting there. The US diplomat lived in Kinshasa and worked with John Kelley, the chief of the office, and with US ambassador James C. Swan, to track the DRC through the lens of US foreign policy and work on diplomacy in that part of the world.

That day started a professional relationship between MJ and Anton. MJ became a key source in eastern Congo. In official documents, MJ's moniker was "Butch." MJ demanded that they use encrypted email. Anton rolled his eyes and said he couldn't understand the need for security in eastern Congo. "Looking back now, he was right to be security conscious," said Anton. "He was always security conscious. He was the most careful contact I've ever had."

Their professional conversations revolved around demobilization, disarmament, and repatriation of the FDLR. Their goal was to get FDLR soldiers to leave the bush, lay down their arms, and return to society. The PPR could work at that, but if the US State Department and United Nations were involved, it would take the conversations to another level.

As a source for the US State Department, MJ's information was used in intelligence briefings. "He was the source of a lot of our knowledge and it influenced a lot of our policy as it related to eastern Congo, particularly as it related to the FDLR," said Anton, who realized that other diplomats in Rwanda didn't understand the group. Anton wrote a cable, as briefs are still called in the diplomatic community, using MJ's intelligence, and it became "the cable" that shaped the diplomats' thinking.

The more Anton trusted MJ's research and work, the better friends they became. When MJ visited Kinshasa, Anton picked him up on a motorcycle and they went to Anton's home for dinner with his wife and children. "He was as good of a friend as I had in the Congo," said Anton.

MJ met both Kelley and Swan. As they worked toward repatriation, UN officials felt that they were getting played, and FDLR leaders were anxious, Anton said. MJ was a calming force, interpreting and communicating to bring the groups together. He knew the nuances. Knowing the nuances is what it takes to make peace.

ℤ ℤ ℤ ℤ

It's not always easy to recognize a combatant. MJ was often surprised to find that the leader of a rebel group or person responsible for violence was actually an unassuming man.

In their conversations, these men would sometimes take credit for the violence and other times take credit for making peace. MJ listened, with the intent of humanizing them and taking them seriously. Even when he questioned, he did so graciously. Tim Lind watched MJ's deep commitment to the idea that if you approach others as humans, you can work through significant differences.

Serge Lungele had been part of the repatriation program since its beginnings in 2006 and was manager of the project from 2008 to 2012. PPR used church networks in the African Great Lakes region to work with the governments of Burundi, Tanzania, Uganda, Rwanda, and the DRC so that people viewed as combatants, as part of an armed group, could come out of the forest and return home. The program was started by a Norwegian and funded by that country's foreign ministry, covering PPR's administrative costs. MCC helped provide food and medical care. MJ advocated for people to return with enough food for a month rather than just several days.

Pursuing permission for the return to Rwanda of someone who was part of the FDLR or another armed group took coordination with the National Commission for Refugees and

MONUSCO. A steering committee helped set up strategies and worked out the details.

While MJ was good at being the administrator of programs that provided food and school fees from an international non-governmental organization, it was this work of repatriation and peacemaking that ignited his passion and intellect. As MJ reported back to MCC and made connections with others in the DRC, visitors from the United States, Great Britain, and Germany started coming to see PPR's innovative work. "We started receiving big people coming that just wanted to understand what the program was doing," Serge said.

What they had been doing since 2008 was making it possible for families who were part of the FDLR to go home to Rwanda.

In 2008–9, the program made way for 1,057 civilians and 298 combatants to go home.

The next year, 4,289 civilians and 853 combatants were released by the FDLR to return.

In all, more than 23,000 civilians and 1,600 combatants returned home between 2008 and 2015 because of the program.

In 2013, PPR started organizing big ceremonies as part of the process. Singing, dancing, and speeches preceded the exit from the DRC. MJ was part of these ceremonies, sometimes in his white polo shirt and sometimes wearing a sports coat. No matter what he was wearing, he fully engaged with those around him.

On December 30, 2013, the FDLR announced it would end its military operations but continue its political struggle for power in Rwanda, according to an MCC report. In May, 105 combatants had voluntarily demobilized in North Kivu with about 500 dependents.

In June, another ceremony took place in South Kivu involving eighty-three combatants dubbed "guerrillas" by *New York*

Times reporter Somini Sengupta in the paper's coverage of the ceremony.

The event meant something in both political and military terms. Diplomats and others were calling for a military solution to bring peace by removing the FDLR from eastern Congo. There was pressure to attack the FDLR. MJ and others in the PPR were trying to respond peacefully.

Powerful people took part in this ceremony. Diplomats arrived and left via helicopter. MJ and Anton Jongeneel, who was among them, pretended not to know each other so as not to put MJ in any danger.

It was a contentious time among those working with the FDLR, whose leaders were anxious. MJ became a key figure in the conversations because of how well he knew the FDLR. He could explain the nuances and keep the factions talking. MJ was invited to more meetings. "When we realized how much he knew, we put him in front of the Special Envoy for the Great Lakes, US senator Russ Feingold," Anton said. As they met on a boat on Lake Kivu, Feingold wanted to learn from MJ about armed groups and security in the region. According to Anton, Feingold told him, "C'mon, Michael. Tell me what you've got."

Publicly, Feingold was calling for a military solution. "People involved in genocide, who are included in this group, are not entitled to dialogue," he was quoted as saying in a *New York Times* story.[6]

MJ was looking for money to fund the ongoing peacemaking work. In an email to NPR reporter Greg Warner, he said that he and others at PPR were hoping to come up with $600,000 from the US Agency for International Development (USAID) and others for an annual budget, since the Norwegians had just pulled their funding.[7] The organization didn't get that. MCC upped its funding as PPR continued the work of demobilization.

When MJ arrived in eastern DRC, MCC programs were spending less than $100,000 per year in the country. In less than three years, that number grew to more than $1 million. "This isn't automatically a good thing," MJ wrote in a report, "but it shows at the very least the growing capacity of partners to implement larger projects and MCC's capacity to make funds available to these partners."[8]

Yet MJ was able to demonstrate the need and how the money was being used effectively, including for this demobilization work. As MJ wrote in an email thread, "There is a good reintegration program that is set up for [former combatants] when they get back to Rwanda. It includes civics lessons, job training, literacy programs for those that need them, etc. They get reintegration kits and money to facilitate their transition. While I can't say we still have contact with all of them, our quarterly follow-up visits to a selection of the returnees have been very positive. It doesn't take much to make life significantly better outside of the Congolese bush."[9]

ℕ ℕ ℕ ℕ

MJ built a life he relished in the DRC.

At times, he struggled with the loneliness of working in a faraway country, yet as he made friends, he found the comfort of community, even if the comforts of home weren't the same. He would stream movies on his computer or get up in the middle of the night to watch his beloved Pittsburgh Steelers play an American football game. As usual, he often charmed women around him and occasionally dated some of them, though no one filled the hole in his heart left by his breakup with Hannah.

He didn't have a faithful companion as he'd had with his childhood dogs, but he raised chickens, rabbits, and guinea pigs in pens he had built with the help of others. Over time, his flock grew from four chickens to more than thirty. He told family and friends on a vlog he sent in September 2013 that he also had three rabbits and a dozen guinea pigs. His family and friends could hear roosters crowing in the background of the video he recorded of himself showing maps and photos as he responded to their questions, along with background music by R.E.M.

A crowing rooster also helped mark the entry of Patrick Maxwell to the country the same month MJ sent that video. As MJ focused on work related to the FDLR, Patrick focused on advocacy related to agriculture and internally displaced persons in the region, though over time their work overlapped and evolved. Patrick had attended Goshen College, and was born in Uganda when his parents were serving as country representatives for MCC. He had some African experience, and the two shared a number of mutual friends. "The Mennonite world is a pretty small one," said Patrick.

MJ and Patrick met up in Kigali, Rwanda, and filled the seven-hour drive to Bukavu with rich conversation. Patrick, still jet-lagged, fell into bed in his new bedroom next to the rooster pen. Early the next morning, the rooster started crowing around four thirty. It would crow and then quiet, and through the first five or six cycles, Patrick faded in and out of sleep. Then Patrick heard scuffling and grunting.

He got up and looked out to see MJ, wearing only flip-flops and boxer shorts, chasing the rooster around the pen with a machete, swinging wildly at the animal. Patrick watched, not sure how to process what he was seeing in this strange new land. MJ wanted Patrick to get a good night's rest, and the rooster was thwarting that.

The night watchman heard what was happening and sprinted toward the pen. He stood staring slack-jawed for several minutes at the nearly naked MJ trying to kill a rooster. The man persuaded MJ to stop, promising that he would kill the rooster that day and they could eat it for supper.

"And it was delicious," Patrick said.

The animals that were part of what MJ called "Sharp Farms" were a peaceable kingdom, in a way, according to Patrick. MJ had a vision for how they could thrive and grow together. But then the rabbits and guinea pigs died, perhaps contracting something from the chickens. The young men then got rid of all the chickens too. They tried to raise just rabbits for a while, but didn't succeed. Patrick and MJ didn't eat the rabbits, but they learned that staff members were happy to receive them as gifts.

The two men lived together and worked in the same office, though both traveled a lot for their roles. Being roommates in eastern Congo is different from being roommates in Boston or Chicago. The baseline stress level is higher, said Patrick. But they got along well. If they were both in Bukavu, they'd come home, have some whiskey, watch a movie on the laptop, and cook dinner. Sometimes when they traveled together, Patrick would ride on the back of MJ's motorcycle, which at some point he upgraded to a 250 cc Yamaha.

Patrick saw the stress of international life and work bother all the expats, including himself. "I would say it was quite normal for expat workers in Congo to hit some sort of burnout," he said. MJ got away, even traveling to Germany to see Sgt. Bob, Hannah, and those at Hausgemeinschaft.

Though raising animals at the compound, which they came to call "Chez Awesome," wasn't ultimately successful, what MJ did foster well was friendships. Vanessa Hershberger arrived as an MCC worker in DRC in the beginning of 2015 and came to live in the compound, which didn't have electricity for six weeks. They played a lot of Up and Down the River with headlamps.

As he had done with others in the past, he sat with her after a hard day. "He could be an incredibly compassionate person," she said.

She also saw him fight for others, to help them get what they deserved or needed. She saw him get angry and heard him critique his ungracious responses to demands for bribes to accomplish something in Congolese culture.

"He was fully human," said Vanessa.

₪ ₪ ₪ ₪

MJ got the chance not just to practice peacebuilding, but to teach it to others.

Shortly after he arrived in Africa in 2012, he was off to the Great Lakes Peacebuilding Institute, a monthlong gathering in Burundi. MJ was one of about twenty people, including other MCCers, participating in the program. The content wasn't new to MJ, but the context was. He was able to network with others doing that work in the region. MJ quickly made friends, joking with others and interacting energetically. And in a role-playing exercise during one workshop, MJ even had an opportunity to showcase his theatrical talents.

Mulanda "Jimmy" Juma, the peacebuilding coordinator for MCC in southern Africa, based in Johannesburg, who taught two weeks of the institute, said, "We quickly became good friends. He was a very happy person. He immediately adapted himself to the context as if he was living in this context for many years."

The next year, MJ was asked to present. Drawing from dozens of articles and scans of books on his computer, he created five days of material on theories of conflict. Though many of his background sources were in German, drawn from his master's degree program in Marburg, MJ presented the class in French. The PowerPoint presentation covered how social identities shape action, the complications and dilemmas caused by conflicts, the various theories on how to achieve peace, and how narratives play a role in shaping our lives and actions.

He wasn't just performing—as he passionately and graciously taught those gathered, he was planting seeds. In the past year, he had at times been overwhelmed by how to build a capacity for peace in a country where it was so difficult to cultivate.

Mennonites, particularly those of MJ's generation, grow up believing that problems can be solved without violence. Doing peacebuilding work is complicated. John Paul Lederach, a Mennonite and a longtime international peacebuilder, compares it to tunneling through a volcano: "Pacifism doesn't make any sense if you are removed from where the challenges are," he explained to me.

Peacebuilders have to offer alternatives to violence. MJ was living and working among militia groups who had chosen weapons. "What you're trying to figure out is ways that can be reduced and stopped and trying to provide protection to the most vulnerable," John Paul said. "What it means is making relationships with people who are very different from you."

When MJ met with leaders of the FDLR, he listened and tried to reshape their narrative. As he stood in front of others at the peacebuilding institute, he tried to give them a foundation of how to approach peacebuilding as a craft.

"Michael Sharp's life in Congo left seeds," said Jimmy. "He left seeds in the Congo and those seeds are growing. Those men and women that he worked with, that he coached and trained, are continuing with his work."

Out of that training, a women-led organization called Oasis de la Culture emerged to put their training into practice and do peacebuilding work in South Kivu province amid ongoing violence to help those in need. The group, which is still a partner of MCC and ECC-MERU, uses agriculture, growing crops and raising animals, as they engage in conflict resolution and build peaceful communities.

Buloze Bugonge, a mother of five and a survivor of militia violence, was displaced in South Kivu province and struggling to recover from an auto crash when Oasis de la Culture gave her corn flour, salt, beans, and vegetable oil. Over time, as she was able to do more, she got a hoe and seeds. "Because of the food we are getting from our field through Oasis de la Culture, we now look like people who have life," she said in an MCC publication in May 2021. "The food grown in the field was very helpful because prices of food in the market had increased because of Covid. This food from the field was very helpful to me and my family."[10]

The figurative seeds of peace that MJ planted continue to grow, sometimes via actual seeds.

಄ ಄ ಄ ಄

In the camps with people who were displaced from their homes, MJ encountered others' pain and responded with compassion.

On one visit, he encountered a boy lying on the ground at the Mubimbi camp for displaced persons near Minova on the shore of Lake Kivu. Fourteen-year-old Ciza Bitibiza was in the MCC school fee program. He had an open sore on his backbone and paralysis was setting in. MJ put him in a Land Cruiser and took him to the Heal Africa hospital in Goma. The boy was malnourished and anemic. MJ paid for IVs, medicines, and injections since the boy's parents couldn't afford them. The next day, MJ paid for food for the boy and his father after realizing the hospital hadn't given the malnourished boy anything to eat. In a trip report, MJ wrote that "Heal Africa provided free medical care for everyone (including M23 and FARDC soldiers) during the fighting in Goma, but on this particular day, nothing will be done for this kid wasting away on their bed unless a white dude gets mad at them. It's not a good day to mess with me."

It was similar to the good Samaritan parable Jesus told in Luke 10 about understanding who your neighbor is. Even on the other side of the globe from where you were born and raised, MJ believed, you can tend a boy as your neighbor. Yet Serge Lungele says that MJ was the only one who would go as far as he did, taking a boy to the hospital, demanding treatment, and paying for treatment.

MJ told his family that because he was able to offer money to help send a preteen girl to school, her family didn't need her to marry. "One life at a time," he said.

In Sange, a city of about forty thousand in South Kivu, MCC paid the school fees of 205 orphans, many of whom lost parents when a tanker truck overturned and exploded in 2010, killing more than four hundred people. The fees were twenty-five to thirty dollars for the year. The Congolese government had promised to make school free for all children in the country,

Congolese children gather around the camera as MJ visits with them during his time with Mennonite Central Committee. PHOTO USED BY PERMISSION OF MENNONITE CENTRAL COMMITTEE

but it had not happened. In the months after arriving, MJ took part in a distribution of sixty uniforms and pairs of shoes in Sange, plus the payment of fees to nine different schools.

The successful ECC-MERU and MCC project paid for more than three hundred students a year in the camps and cost less than $30,000 a year. The tracking of the students showed that 90 percent of beneficiaries went on to the next grade. MJ worked to expand the project during his stint with MCC. Providing education provided stability. And it planted seeds of hope.

MJ urged the Congolese around him to fight for justice and dignity in their country. Bishop Bulambo Lembelembe Josué, program coordinator for PPR, said MJ "incited us to the noble fight for freedom."

"Michael taught us to strive for peace, justice, and social cohesion," he said. "His fight is our fight today."

₪ ₪ ₪ ₪

In mid-2012, about the same time that MJ had arrived in the DRC, the International Criminal Court issued a warrant for Sylvestre Mudacumura's arrest. Mudacumura was a wanted war criminal, and during his time in the DRC, MJ worked to bring him in.

Mudacumura was a genocidaire moving about eastern Congo. He had done military training in Germany, was part of the presidential guard of former Rwandan president Juvénal Habyarimana, and even served as the president's personal bodyguard. During the 1994 Rwandan genocide, after Habyarimana's plane was brought down with a missile, Mudacumura is suspected to have played a role in the killing of Tutsis.

The warrant called him the "Alleged Supreme Commander" of the Democratic Forces for the Liberation of Rwanda (FDLR). A 2008 story in *The Guardian* called him Major General and described him as FDLR's overall military commander, who was "wanted by the Rwandan government to face trial for his role as deputy commander of the presidential guard which flew across the country to begin the mass murder in April 1994. Today he is a primary mover behind the killing of Congo's Tutsis."[11]

The Hutu leader occasionally led attacks into Rwanda, but was also responsible for "horrific violence against Congolese civilians, sometimes in alliance with Congolese armed groups," according to Human Rights Watch.[12] Timo Mueller, a friend of MJ's who worked with HRW, said Mudacumura was "like Osama bin Laden for Rwanda."

Mudacumura was charged with nine counts of war crimes between January 2008 and September 2010, including murder, mutilation, cruel treatment, torture, rape, destruction of property, attacking civilians, and outrage upon personal dignity. The FDLR attacked at least half a dozen villages in the Kivu provinces in coalition with the Congolese army FARDC and Rwanda Defense Forces (RDF).

There was growing pressure to bring in Mudacumura. It's likely that this was discussed with former US senator Feingold, who couldn't officially order a raid but may have had the authority to spur one. The UN Force Intervention Brigade was ready to drop a bomb on Mudacumura and wanted MJ's help. But MJ didn't want to be involved in an approach that would kill someone—even someone who had enacted a genocide. He could have taken the easy route by enabling a military attack to kill the rebel leader and collecting the $5 million reward that had been offered in 2013 by US secretary of state John Kerry. But MJ was making the case to FDLR leaders that if Mudacumura turned himself in, his family could be kept safe. He was making the case that giving Mudacumura an option to turn himself in would keep the aging soldier, who had recently turned sixty, alive as well.

Mudacumura's family had gone to Germany for their safety, but he remained with his troops. MJ, as an expert on the FDLR who was quietly collaborating with the US State Department, was sent as an envoy to try to persuade Mudacumura to turn himself in. The general had seven circles of people around him. MJ got to the last circle on a secretive visit. Negotiating with Mudacumura was risky, sensitive, and challenging.

MJ wanted to do this peaceably and spent months working through the circles around the general. At times, he got very close. "We were so sure it was going to happen we had started discussing how to distribute the reward money," said Anton Jongeneel, the State Department envoy in the DRC who worked with MJ. They discussed giving the money to MCC.

MJ was relatively quiet about what he was trying to do, but he did tell a few friends that he was getting close. MJ wasn't chasing the money. He never had. He was trying to wage peace in eastern Congo and relishing a challenge as big as this one. Having Mudacumura out of the system would have done that. "They were so close to succeeding in that matter. It could have been a game changer," said MJ's coworker Emmanuel Billay.

Though he came close, MJ wasn't able to convince Mudacumura to turn himself in to authorities.

An FBI agent approached MJ's father at MJ's memorial service. John, not realizing who she was, thought, "Another one of MJ's girlfriends." She told John that MJ was the only person she had met who didn't want the reward money. He just wanted peaceful justice for the violence Mudacumura had wrought.

Mudacumura stayed on the run until September 2019. Government forces killed him and his lieutenants in the Rutshuru territory. Possibly killed by his own men as the enemy closed in, he died the violent death that MJ had tried to convince him to avoid.

What do we stand for as a global community? What are the responsibilities for our common fate in a world that is simultaneously coming together and coming apart—and how do we exercise those responsibilities? How do we strike the balance between growth and development, equality and opportunity, human rights and human security?

—**KOFI ANNAN**, _Interventions_

NINE

United Nations, Divided People

IN EARLY OCTOBER 2014, Emilie Serralta, who was in her second year on the United Nations Group of Experts for the DRC, met with a Congolese source in Bukavu who said, "Do you know that American guy? He knows so much about the FDLR. He goes and meets with them."

That led to her to call MJ and meet him in a restaurant in Bukavu. He spoke quickly and impressed her with his knowledge and passion. Emilie had been coordinator of the Group of Experts the prior year and was still part of the group.

The UN hired members annually for the Group of Experts who do research on behalf of the UN Security Council. "Our bosses were the Security Council and they set out our work plan," said Dan Fahey, who was on the group in 2013 and 2014. He was an American researcher who became an expert on the Allied Democratic Forces, a rebel group that began in western

Uganda and expanded into eastern DRC. Dan had worked in the DRC since 2005 and had done his doctorate there. "I was passionate about wanting to do this job to make a difference for Congo," Dan said.

The Security Council issues mandates for Groups of Experts for a range of functions in countries across the world. Sometimes a Group of Experts will operate in a country for a few years and then the conflict or violations of international law abate and the UN no longer issues a mandate. The Security Council established a committee in 2000 to investigate exploitation of natural resources in the DRC. In 2004, it added oversight of arms transfers because of the armed groups that were springing up in the region after the Rwandan genocide. Then the Group of Experts was asked to oversee freezing of assets and travel bans for people in those groups as a means to curb their activities.

The Security Council mandates Groups of Experts to gather and submit information on the extent to which sanctions are working and potentially recommend new sanctions. The experts are the eyes and ears, the people in the field, providing information to others throughout the organization. Their reports also carry weight because of how they do research and investigations.

In the DRC, the Group of Experts each year was composed of six people with no more than one person from a single country. In 2014, Dan, an American, was an expert on armed groups, as was Emilie, a French woman. Four others in the group focused on natural resources, arms and ammunition tracking, and human rights violations. An office staff of several people assisted the group by serving as drivers and translators.

MJ learned more from Emilie about the particulars of being on the Group of Experts and was interested in the job. He was highly respected in the diplomatic community, as well as those who worked for NGOs and the UN. "I remember hearing most about his work with the FDLR and his ability to connect with combatants and people who are part of the group and persuade them to leave the bush, to participate in peace talks," said Ida Sawyer, Central Africa Director for Human Rights Watch and an expert on the DRC from her years of work there. A North American using personal relationships to do that kind of work was rare, and he seemed to be independent and able to figure things out on his own, she said. Expats in the Congo often work for an organization, follow its lead, and live in a bubble. "Michael seemed to chart his own path and didn't need to follow the pack," she said.

MJ sent documents to apply for the job. Emilie recommended MJ to Dan, who was then the coordinator. After reviewing MJ's curriculum vitae, Dan recommended that the New York office take on MJ, who was thirty-two years old. In general, the UN office was reluctant to hire someone so young, and MJ had a baby face that made him look even younger. Yet MJ wanted the job and had clear qualifications.

"I think it seemed to be an intellectual challenge for him and he really liked challenges," said Emilie.

It was a natural next step for someone who had come to the DRC and made a difference. MJ was motivated and, as he often did, was asking what would come next after his MCC term ended in summer 2015.

In an ongoing WhatsApp conversation in 2013 and 2014, MJ and Sgt. Bob unpacked their vocational questions. Sgt. Bob was considering becoming a firefighter in the western United States. They joked about opening a Waffle House in Germany or an ice cream shop in Congo, or about starting a religion.

MJ wanted to stay in the DRC and continue some form of the work that he loved. He told friend Justin Ramer that his life in the Congo was complicated, but he delighted in it. MJ told

Justin that he had spent time in about forty countries and that the problems were real everywhere, whether they're armed groups or the daily grind of a nine-to-five job in the United States. "It's not like I was forced to come here. I chose it, and I'm totally happy," he wrote, signing the email "Dr. Congo."

ꉈ ꉈ ꉈ ꉈ

MJ, always the charmer, often had a girlfriend or someone who wished to be.

He dated often and easily. As he traveled, he would sometimes strike up an online relationship with a woman in the city he would be visiting and then spend several intense days with her while there. He was looking for someone who was willing to be a citizen of the world, unafraid to travel and even live and work in unconventional spots such as the Congo.

By fall 2014, as MJ was leaning into working for the UN, MJ had fallen deeply in love with a European woman working in the DRC. He told friends that they would soon need tuxes for their wedding.

But she broke off the relationship and broke his heart. His pain intermingled with his work and his wrestling with vocational questions of what came next. In late 2014, Ben and Beth Weisbrod invited MJ and Patrick Maxwell to join them at Bethany Hotel, a lush resort on the Rwandan side of Lake Kivu. The Weisbrods were veteran MCCers who had become area directors for central and western Africa in August 2014. They had gotten to know the young men and heard their tales of trying to raise rabbits, of the bombing of Goma by M23. Ben and Beth were based in Rwanda but traveled frequently to visit the MCC workers in seven countries, including the DRC.

As they visited in December 2014, Ben could see MJ's melancholy and need for rest. His broken heart, and his sadness over missing Suzanne and Tim Lind after they had left MCC and returned to the United States, was evident. MJ said he needed a combination of quiet space and mentoring.

Those days at the resort included long conversations at the edge of the lake, as well as kayaking, hiking, and card playing. MJ told Ben about the possibility of joining the Group of Experts. He also told Ben and Beth he wanted to be a father and was considering writing and teaching, as his father was doing. Yet the possibility of peacebuilding in a new context intrigued him. His understanding of armed groups, conflict, and even weaponry could help him in that role.

Ben was hopeful that MJ would become the MCC country representative in Nigeria, where the Boko Haram situation was intensifying. Yet he also understood MJ's quest for another job and supported it. MJ wasn't content with having laid a foundation. According to Ben, he wanted to work on the superstructure that went beyond the foundation.

₪ ₪ ₪ ₪

Dan Fahey had recommended that MJ become part of the Group of Experts for the 2015 mandate. He saw that MJ had a deep and profound love for the Congo, an appreciation of its history and people, and a sadness at seeing a wonderful country mired in dysfunction and violence.

They talked by phone after Dan decided not to rejoin. "He was the perfect guy to be on the group," Dan said.

He told MJ that it was probably the best job he'd ever had, and the worst. He had loved the freedom and the importance of the work, but not the bureaucracy and the lack of interest in the security of those on the group.

Dan learned that the UN wasn't putting MJ on the 2015 group, in an effort to include more Africans and women. The group would be without an American. Dan was at the UN in New York and then traveled to Washington, D.C., to debrief with US officials. He told people on the Congo desk of the State Department that Michael Sharp was up for the group, but wasn't being selected. "I would really encourage you to reconsider. He's the kind of guy you need on the group," Dan told them.

Rejection and hope swirled together for MJ. He was coping with the loss of a relationship as he worked on a grand possibility. Ben Weisbrod watched MJ respond with grace and self-awareness as he processed the losses and what could yet emerge.

At the US State Department and the UN, the conversations had continued. Something, somewhere changed. MJ got the call. The job came through.

On March 5, MJ received word that he was joining the Group of Experts. A week later, on March 12, 2015, he was officially nominated.

MJ told Sgt. Bob it was scary and awesome all at the same time. He would officially become a contractor for the UN as an armed groups expert on the Group of Experts, earning almost as much in a month as he'd earned annually with MCC.

He was an American who knew the DRC and was a peacemaker. He had the skills to make a difference. Julie Jolles, who worked as a foreign service officer for the State Department, said, "You'd scratch your eyes out to get an applicant this good."

₪ ₪ ₪ ₪

Just as he had with the Military Counseling Network and Mennonite Central Committee, MJ joined the work of the United Nations to try to do good in the world. The church organizations were tiny compared to the global organization, and the work took on a different meaning and level of intensity.

He joined a group coordinated by Gaston Gramajo—the primary point of contact for the UN and others outside the group and the one who handled more administrative tasks. Zobel Behalal, Rupert Cook, Koenraad de Swaef, and Emmanuel Viret were the other members. It was an entirely new group to the DRC, with Dan Fahey, Emilie Serralta, and four others leaving.

MJ had already been talking to Emilie, Dan, and Jason Stearns, a former group member who is one of the preeminent experts on the DRC and wrote *Dancing in the Glory of Monsters* about the wars there. MJ was expected to start in April and went to the UN's New York headquarters for training. Kelvin Ong, chief of the branch of the United Nations Security Council that oversaw the Groups of Experts, welcomed the seventy-one experts on twelve panels. MJ was officially a consultant, and Ong told them the UN couldn't tell them what to say in their reports, though they were part of the UN.

In a similar way, MJ's notes indicate that the group's role was to give information to the Security Council, but the experts

MJ, in this photo taken by Zaida, is dressed up for United Nations meetings.
PHOTO USED BY PERMISSION OF MORESBY FAMILY

should never say that the Security Council would act on them in any way. Part of the work was interacting with member states to gather information, and those relationships were important. Sanctions work best with international cooperation and links with envoys, peacekeeping, and humanitarian aid. Ong told them that as experts they were all known, and they couldn't present themselves as something else. "Rwanda has known who you are for a long time," MJ wrote, referring to himself.

MJ learned not only how to fill out paperwork for reimbursement, but also how to request use of satellites and radar to aid investigations. Conversations also covered working with Interpol and other groups and officials.

UN human rights officials outlined how experts could help MONUSCO and UNICEF protect children from being recruited into armed groups and how the experts monitor six violations, including abductions and attacks on schools and hospitals. Other briefings covered how armed groups were smuggling gold and other natural resources. "Minerals keep the war going," MJ wrote in his notes.

MJ was skilled at gathering information in the field. After all, he was the one who often said, "You can always listen." Yet in working for the UN, there were standards for conducting an international investigation. His notes mention chain of custody, labeling protocols, how to conduct interviews. "Each person has only their own view of the events; investigators need to put these many views together to create the whole picture," he noted.

The normal pattern for a member of the Group of Experts is to spend about six weeks in the country and then two or so weeks elsewhere. The experts often work independently both in their home country and the DRC. Then twice a year, the DRC group gathers in Brindisi, a city on the Adriatic coast of southern Italy, to write its reports.

Though MJ's passport had been well used before this, his work with the UN was soon to have him using more planes and taxis than ever before. Since his home address was his parents' in Hesston, Kansas, his commute in April 2015 was Wichita to Minneapolis, Minneapolis to New York, New York to Paris, Paris to Kinshasa, Kinshasa to Goma—all by plane. While he was in the DRC on that trip, he used a combination of planes and boats to travel among Goma, Beni, and Bukavu.

When he returned home in mid-June, it was Kigali to Amsterdam, Amsterdam to Brussels, Brussels to Atlanta, and Atlanta to Wichita over four days. Two weeks later, he headed back to the DRC, where he stayed with other expats in a house in Goma overlooking Lake Kivu.

That pattern continued over much of the next two years as occasionally different routes garnered more stamps in the extra sewn-in pages of his passport.

וגּ וגּ וגּ וגּ

For the first time, MJ was part of the state.

In the past, Mennonites were urged to avoid holding office or working in the government out of humility and a distrust of power.

Andy Gingerich saw his friend offering an alternative. "Could it be that the larger systems and structures in the world need to be served and redeemed the same way that people do?" Andy told me as he reflected on MJ's work. "Perhaps it's possible to enter the political/government/legal arena and not lose your humility, not seek personal power, not exalt yourself, and instead be willing to serve and suffer within it as you seek to redeem it."

In a world that is more connected than ever, it's important to wrestle with how to humbly work to serve others and perhaps be part of larger systems and structures, Andy said.

He had hoped to keep figuring out these kinds of questions with his friend, whom he watched throw himself at the world while holding on to his values, upbringing, and heritage.

MJ was driven by his beliefs, but also by finding "new paths to peace," said Andy.

Though the United Nations isn't a government, it is a governing force composed of the governments who are members. It also has an armed force.

The UN Peacekeepers, as they are called, come from member nations and are intended to be neutral. The United Nations Organization Stabilization Mission in the DR Congo, known as MONUSCO, has about twenty thousand soldiers. It was created in 2010 after an earlier mission. According to the UN, "The new mission has been authorized to use all necessary means to carry out its mandate relating, among other things, to the protection of civilians, humanitarian personnel and human rights defenders under imminent threat of physical violence and to support the Government of the DRC in its stabilization and peace consolidation efforts."[1]

The UN peacekeeping efforts and response to issues for internally displaced people and refugees in the DRC came after the Rwandan genocide. The UN stepped forward to take a more active role to keep people safe.[2]

US diplomats had threatened to use the UN army MONUSCO to deal with the FDLR and Sylvestre Mudacumura. MJ was now working for an organization that had a force of "peacekeepers" who could use aggressive action to protect the peace.

That's a rare and uncomfortable spot for a Mennonite to be in, and MJ spent hours talking with his friend Jonathan Moyer about how to navigate it.

"How are you supposed to be the 'quiet in the land' or a peacemaker in a situation where you're advising people with all the guns?" said Jonathan, naming one of the questions with which they wrestled.

Jonathan had grown up Mennonite in eastern Pennsylvania, where MJ's family had been for a time, and was the same age as MJ's sister Erin. As a kid, the story of Clayton Kratz, who disappeared in 1920 while doing relief work for the Molotschna Colony in Ukraine, shaped Jonathan's view of being a Mennonite as being someone who could go into the world rather than just choose to stay home and be the quiet in the land.

After his own college study at Bluffton University, a Mennonite college in Ohio, Jonathan went to Vietnam with Mennonite Central Committee. It was there that he first encountered MJ, who was on an EMU cross-cultural trip in spring 2005 earning credits for three weeks of study as he finished college. He and Jonathan connected on a deep level. "He had this international wanderlust drive thing that I have," Jonathan said. The two would go out at night together in Vietnam.

Jonathan moved to Denver and made friends with other Mennonites, including Erin, who had also moved there. When MJ went to visit his sister, he started spending time with Jonathan, who had become an assistant professor at the Josef Korbel School of International Studies and director of the Frederick S. Pardee Center for International Futures. In that role, he worked for the UN and African Union Development Agency as a consultant.

Mennonites don't have a coherent foreign policy, according to Jonathan. They struggle with the need for an army on a national and international level and even a police force on the local level. Nonresistant Mennonites generally accept the need for armed forces and police, but refuse to join as active participants. Pacifist Mennonites, who like MJ believe nearly any conflict can be solved peaceably, struggle with the existence of armed forces and the actions of those entities.

Now that he was working for the UN, MJ would be asked to do things that could result in outcomes over which he didn't have control, including the possibility that information he gathered would be used to justify military interventions. "The state has a monopoly on legitimate use of force," Jonathan said, explaining that governments can use force to attempt to enact change and that those who work for those systems may be caught up in those efforts.

In the circles MJ was now in, violence is often the first solution. MJ learned to be a chameleon so that he could be taken seriously by those who would have dismissed him out of hand for being a peace-loving Mennonite. He learned to listen first and then suggest that there may be an alternative.

The two wrestled with how they could move in the world, how they could swim in the big ponds that were different from the ones in which they'd grown up. MJ could swim in any of those ponds comfortably, or could at least act comfortable, said Jonathan.

Unlike many other American Mennonites, they didn't choose to live quietly in community. They were trying to apply their beliefs, backed with degrees in which they'd studied peace and its components, in a practical way. That's far more complicated.

MJ was fundamentally Mennonite and loved working at the big puzzle of peace with the UN. Yet he had to process the trade-offs required to make the pieces fit together. Like many Christians, he wrestled with the biblical commandment of how to live with integrity in the world, following a man whose beliefs were so unpopular that he was crucified. In chapter 17 of the gospel of John, Jesus urged Christians to tread lightly on this earth.

"It's hard to know how to be 'in the world and not of the world' when you're really in the world," Jonathan said.

₪ ₪ ₪ ₪

As MJ transitioned into his role with the UN, transitions were also happening with the armed group on which he was an expert.

The FDLR had shrunk in size from about fifteen thousand Rwandan Hutu soldiers after the 1994 genocide to no more than two thousand rebel soldiers, only a small percentage of whom were alive when the genocide happened. The deadline for voluntary disarmament passed as 2015 started. There was growing pressure for the FARDC (the Congolese army) and MONUSCO to attack the group, as they had other armed groups.

The FARDC had indeed battled the armed group M23 in November 2013 and defeated it. Most of the ex-combatants fled to Rwanda and Uganda and didn't return to the DRC. The operation was deemed a success, and the hope was that the national army and MONUSCO could replicate that with other armed groups.

The FARDC and MONUSCO had a joint operation targeting the Allied Democratic Forces in North Kivu in August 2014. This hadn't been successful, and the ADF killed between 350 and 450 civilians between October 2014 and June 2015 in the Beni area of North Kivu province.

As MJ left MCC, he completed a white paper entitled "FDLR Narratives." In it he explained that the FDLR had been seen as "a spoiler to regional peace initiatives" since the mid-1990s and that he wanted to write about the group to shed light on the thinking of those in it to "prevent misunderstanding or situations that can destroy a process or put a practitioner in danger," and point to peacebuilding strategies.[3]

He relied on his interviews and communication with members of the group and highlighted the importance of narrative, just as he had in past peacebuilding efforts in Germany and the Middle East.

He described how the FDLR leaders idealized Rwandan life before the genocide. They accused Paul Kagame, current president of Rwanda, and his Rwandan Patriotic Front rebels of shooting down the plane of then president Juvénal Habyarimana, starting a war that led to their exile. "One notes the lack of any mention of genocide; rather it was a war that broke out after the assassination of a democratically elected president," MJ wrote.[4]

FDLR leadership sometimes brought a copy of the 2005 UN Mapping Report to meetings. The document delineates abuses of human rights by a range of groups in the DRC. The FDLR would point to the ones done by others, not the ones that the UN had noted they had done.

They maintained a narrative that looked back on the good old days and had hope of a powerful return to Rwanda.

In exile, they situated themselves as primarily civilian victims fleeing the military of Rwanda. A colonel had told MJ, "We are here in the forest, living like animals, and simply killed, killed, killed by people on all sides." The FDLR leadership counted twelve military operations against them, with another likely in the coming months. The FDLR leaders said Rwandan forces had attacked them as refugees.

They were willing to await a glorious return to Rwanda and asked for negotiations to broker a power-sharing agreement with President Paul Kagame's government. That wasn't going to happen, and still hasn't as of 2021.

MJ had listened to their stories, their narrative. They urged him to relay what they said, and he could also put it in perspective.

MJ offered a path forward in his white paper:

> If your goal is to reduce the number of FDLR combatants in the forest, you could support the FDLR idea of disarming and cantoning combatants within the Congo or in a third country

while they continue their "political struggle." This does not require that you buy into the FDLR leadership's officially stated goal of bringing about peace to the region or support their request for negotiations with Kigali or even believe they have any intention of giving up more than a few capable individuals. Rather, you are finding a way in which their current strategy and narrative lines up with your goal of removing whatever number of combatants from the forest you can get.[5]

ני ני ני ני

As MJ joined the Group of Experts, he befriended the staff who would work closely with him, just as he had done in the past.

Bally Mutumayi worked as a driver and translator in the office in Goma. MJ invited him to a restaurant, which wasn't common for a group member to do with a Congolese staff member. MJ explained he had worked for a church agency and knew the area well. As they ate chicken and chips, MJ was humble and kind.

Soon, Bally was helping MJ arrange an interview at a hotel where former combatants were imprisoned. MJ and Bally then began visiting a range of prisons in Goma to interview former combatants.

In early September, after a stint in the United States and Canada, MJ helped craft the midterm report in Italy. He and the five others updated the Security Council on armed groups, including the FDLR, natural resources, and violations of international humanitarian law.

The report noted that 339 FDLR combatants had been disarmed but not demobilized. Most of them were in MONUSCO transit camps, along with 1,030 dependents. The document spoke collectively for the group of six. "The Group believes the failure of the voluntary disarmament process was inevitable," the report stated.[6]

The report established the number of prisoners that could be confirmed and delineates who had been captured and who hadn't. No one with a rank of lieutenant colonel or above had been taken into custody. It also outlined how the FDLR continued to illegally tax villages and roads, exploit gold, sell planks and charcoal, and loot vehicles.

Armed groups, including the FDLR, were still recruiting and using children. MONUSCO counted 1,399, including seventy-two girls restored from armed groups in the first eight months of 2015. Most had been forcibly taken by the militias. "They became combatants, escorts for the commanders, servants, tax collectors at mining sites or fetish keepers," said the report.[7]

The midterm report listed recommendations, including an investigation of the general who failed to protect the 350 or more civilians who died in at least fifty separate incidents. ADF combatants killed them, sometimes with machetes, as a tactic in the battle with FARDC soldiers. The group had done dozens of interviews with witnesses, obtained photographs of victims of the massacres, and talked to medical personnel, journalists, and nonprofit workers.

The group found that the FARDC, led by a brigadier general, didn't capture a single ADF combatant. When alerted of ADF positions, the Congolese army claimed it was too dangerous, too dark, or that there weren't enough well-equipped soldiers. At the same time, the group confirmed that FARDC officers were involved in exploiting timber, gold, tin, tantalum, and tungsten.

As political pressure mounted to act against the FDLR, which was avoiding conflict, DRC president Joseph Kabila appointed generals accused of human rights abuses to command the operation for the FARDC. MONUSCO couldn't legally work with the generals, and the operation stalled.

By the time the final report for that Group of Experts was issued in May 2016, the FARDC had been undertaking military operations against a range of armed groups in eastern Congo. MONUSCO had signed a new memo of understanding in February 2016 allowing it to collaborate with the Congolese national army. With 1,400 to 1,600 troops, the FDLR remained the largest armed group in the country, but had been destabilized by both the FARDC and the Mai Mai militia group. The ADF had fractured. The Lord's Resistance Army was coming into the DRC from the Central African Republic and South Sudan to poach elephants and traffic the ivory, committing human rights abuses against civilians as they did so.

The final report highlighted how gold is taken from mines and laundered into the supply chain by armed groups. The group had requested figures from the DRC and neighboring countries and didn't receive them, but they did get statistics from Dubai showing that far more gold was flowing out of the DRC than was being reported. The report lauded how the United Arab Emirates was working on a plan to address the illicit flow of gold and money.

MJ had a large role in crafting the reports for his first Group of Experts appointment. The reports are used by the UN Security Council to track individuals and groups, as well as the overall situation, in a region, but they also are helpful to other nongovernmental organizations because of how they establish facts in what are often fluid situations. MJ told family and friends that he took charge and assured their completion by the UN deadlines.

Soon, he'd be taking on an even larger role.

₪ ₪ ₪ ₪

At the end of his first assignment on the Group of Experts, MJ was able to point to a series of accomplishments.

He had spent sixteen months, from spring 2015 to summer 2016, as part of the group. In his report looking back, he named eighteen armed groups about which he had collected information and data. He had helped provide information on financing, weapons, and other aspects of the conflicts.

"My biggest contributions," he wrote in his end-of-assignment report, "were in regard to the FDLR, where I was able to document external support, continued recruitment in the DRC and abroad (including of children), the use of forced labor, operational plans, inner workings of the organization, active alliances with other armed groups, weapons purchase from the FARDC, continued hindering of the demobilization process, internal conflicts, locations of troop concentrations and major bases, hierarchy, communication codes, refugee card acquisition strategies, tactics for benefiting from humanitarian aid, and extensive income-generating strategies."[8]

He wasn't shy about making recommendations for how to approach the investigatory process in the future. He focused on organization and recognizing how to collaborate with others to fill gaps.

His report is full of questions that guided his own approach to research and thirst for knowledge. He wrote, "In most institutions, you would have a fairly clear job: you'd look at the big picture and plan accordingly, or you'd be a collector in the field acting on those plans and submitting information collected based on that plan, or you'd be an analyst dealing with the information that's coming in, or you'd be writing about that analyzed information for a specific audience. In this job, you have to do all of those things."[9]

As the new mandate started, MJ had proven that he was competent, and he became the coordinator of the group. He was one of the youngest people to hold that position and helped build a team with whom he would do the work.

Christoph Vogel and MJ had met at a party several years earlier, soon after MJ first arrived in the DRC. The two had become friends and would spend hours talking over beers. Christoph was researching patterns of conflict and insecurity in eastern DRC for his doctorate. He had been asked before to consider being on the Group of Experts, but had declined. When MJ asked, Christoph said yes.

Zobel Behalal stayed on the group as an expert on natural resources and finance issues, joined by Roberto Sollazzo from Italy. David Zounmenou of Benin joined to focus on arms and ammunition trafficking. Zaida Catalán became the expert on human rights.

In the fall of 2016, as they began their work together, MJ was their *primus inter pares*, Latin for "first among equals." Yet he made it clear that he had hopes for how they would collaborate not just to produce a midterm report and final report, but to do even more. In the previous mandate, the group wrote two reports and two progress updates in sixteen months. He told this group he expected they would complete two reports and ten progress updates in twelve months. The sanctions committee wanted to pay closer attention to the DRC and the confidential updates, which didn't require the same standard of evidence as a report. In the previous year, an update and confidential annex were leaked, jeopardizing an investigation and putting a witness's life in danger. "We won't be making those mistakes again, as far as we can help it," MJ wrote to his colleagues.

Much of what he recommended to others in the group was the same as what he had recommended in his end-of-term report. He urged the other experts to do hundreds of interviews and organize them well. He outlined a planning, analysis, and writing process that resulted in clear and focused recommendations and reports. He urged them to respect the writing process and told them it would take many rewrites to get it right.

₪ ₪ ₪ ₪

As MJ started his second mandate, his focus was on the situation in Beni territory, where hundreds had died since fall 2014.

The Allied Democratic Forces continued to battle the FARDC national army in North Kivu province near Virunga National Park, near the cities of Beni and Butembo. The core of the group, with several hundred individuals in the forest, was Ugandan and was recruiting in neighboring countries by promising free education and high-paying jobs. The reality, according to those who escaped or were captured, was a strict society in which they were forced into hard labor or worse.

In his individual research plan, MJ made it clear that Beni was his primary focus and that his goal was to explain the complicated situation and various armed groups. "People are starting to understand much better the dynamics, but it will take a concerted effort to bring these things to light in a report," he wrote.[10]

To this end, MJ and the other experts conducted hundreds of interviews.

They went to camps to interview people who had escaped from an armed group and were being helped by an organization.

They went to offices of government officials, sometimes meeting with more than one at a time.

Sometimes the interviews were with expats like themselves who were researching or working in the DRC, and they met at hotels, restaurants, or bars. Former members of the Group of Experts still working in the country provided invaluable information.

Many of the interviews were done in French, Swahili, or another language. Typing up notes from an interview done in one's nonnative language, regardless of whether it was with an interpreter, is tedious, but MJ wanted the experts on the group to be more diligent in doing so than in some previous groups.

Those who had escaped the armed groups, whether it was ADF, FDLR, or others, told chilling tales of what they had witnessed. Sometimes they shared photos of what they had seen, but most often it was a verbal account of an incident or time with a group.

MJ's interviewing skills are clear by the breadth of his reports. He listed nicknames and aliases of those leading groups. A number of his reports noted the location of "Muda," as Sylvestre Mudacumura continued to escape capture. MJ heard regular reports of where the elusive war criminal was located.

MJ's interviews covered operations, supplies, training, and communications. Some interviews covered where gold was being mined and sold. As alliances among armed groups changed, those being interviewed helped the experts understand the changing scene. A day might have one interview or dozens.

Investigating and creating regular reports about the DRC was challenging work and a puzzle that MJ loved. But this wasn't like a two-dimensional puzzle of a pretty picture that lays on a table until someone puts all the pieces together. The puzzle the Group of Experts wrestled with in the DRC was one where the pieces change how they fit together and even layer on top of each other over time. In some cases, such as how the FDLR operated in eastern DRC, clear patterns emerge in time, but then a new situation emerges and becomes a mystery to be solved. The experts were working to both document the details and explain the big picture.

The work of the members of the Group of Experts, particularly those focused on armed groups, was to document weaponry and ammunition and what group was responsible. In early December 2015, MJ texted a friend to say that he was following the military as it cleared new areas and that the sooner he could get to a former rebel position, the better evidence he could get. His goal was to slip into villages right after the fighting ended. "It's more dangerous than interviews, but offers much more concrete evidence," he told a friend. "Basically, rebel groups leave all kinds of interesting things behind when they abandon positions in a hurry: bullet casings, cell phones, letters, sim cards, etc. All of those things are gold for me."

A few days before, he and another expert were in a village with 150 empty huts. Those who had lived there had fled the fighting. "I could hear the wind blowing, the goats and chickens made a bit of noise from time to time, but that was it! So eery," he said.

On August 13, 2016, people armed with machetes, axes, and Kalashnikov-style rifles moved through the area of Rwangoma near the city of Beni, killing thirty-six people. Group members were able to get to the area two days later to collect evidence and talk to witnesses, who in their still-fresh trauma gave varying accounts of what the killers were wearing. Group members confirmed thirty-six deaths, thirty-three by ax or machete and three by shooting, but said the number of dead was likely higher. Some of the bodies were still lying where they had been killed.

₪ ₪ ₪ ₪

In early November, the Group of Experts prepared its midterm report for the UN Security Council.

The six gathered in Brindisi, Italy, to draft the document, which is usually about twenty pages of text with supporting documentation. The members would send their material to the coordinator and then work together over the course of a week to discuss what should be included in the report. They followed a schedule to discuss the investigations and how to handle them.

In order for information to be included in the report, it had to meet the standard of evidence. Citations and facts needed to be verifiable and based on verifiable documents or first-hand, on-site observations by the experts.[11] The group members challenged each other on what should be included and pushed each other when the work wasn't strong enough, which can be a humbling and difficult process for an expert.

The midterm report updated many of the recurring issues found in previous reports, including the ADF in Beni territory, the FDLR weakening in North Kivu, and the challenge of tracing gold as it was exploited for profit and crime. The document noted the arrest of several military leaders of the FDLR and internal divisions resulting in a split into a new group called Conseil national pour le renouveau et la démocratie-Ubwiyunge (CNRD), leaving holes in the original FDLR. Desertion was on the rise and the group was trying to enlist and train new recruits. The narrative on the FDLR and new offshoot covered four and a half pages in the midterm report.

The report documented violations of human rights and international humanitarian law in the Beni and Rutshuru territories of North Kivu, including attacks on civilians and the use of child soldiers. Arms embargo violations as the Sudan People's Liberation Movement/Army in Opposition entered the DRC were delineated as well. The reporting over twenty pages in the document was clear and concise. Another sixty-seven pages of documents, photos, and supporting information were well organized.

The large underlying issue named in the first paragraph of the report was the political tension caused by DRC president Joseph Kabila delaying the elections that were to happen in December 2016. Kabila had been in power for two terms and under the constitution was to yield to a new president. Yet he was holding on to power and postponing the elections. That was leading to protests in which civilians were being killed or arrested in Kinshasa.

Kabila had taken office as a shy, reclusive leader thrust into the spotlight after his father's death. He learned French and slowly assumed the full power that had been given to him as the leader of an African country with immense natural resources. He did not invest the earnings from those into the country in any way. The DRC has one of the lowest per capita incomes in the world. Its infrastructure is in shambles. Kabila did forge agreements with other countries, but mostly to secure his power or the mining rights of the country to line his pockets.

Kabila had come to power in 2001 ten days after the assassination of his father Laurent-Désiré Kabila. The elder Kabila had been a soldier and a government official, and had even assisted Che Guevara in 1965 when he came to the Congo to try to bring about a revolution as had happened in Cuba. Laurent Kabila was a Marxist whose army overran the country in 1997 and overthrew Mobutu Sese Seko, the dictator who had called the country Zaire. Kabila became president in 1997 and withstood two wars before he was shot in January 2001.

Who was behind the elder Kabila's assassination? Some would say operatives from Rwanda, Zimbabwe, Angola, or even the United States. Others would say it was generals he had fired for performance in a battle. The investigation into Laurent Kabila's death arrested 135 people and put them before a military tribunal.

"As so often in the Congo, the truth may never be known," writes Jason Stearns in *Dancing in the Glory of Monsters: The Collapse of the Congo and the Great War of Africa*. "Sometimes it seems that crossing the border into the Congo one abandons any sort of Archimedean perspective on truth and becomes caught up in a web of rumors and allegations, as if the country itself were the stuff of some post-modern fiction."[12]

MJ gathers with program workers and those receiving food and farming aid. PHOTO USED BY PERMISSION OF MENNONITE CENTRAL COMMITTEE

The courage to die for their beliefs is given only to those who have had the courage to live for them. The final victory over their terror of pain and physical death is the last of a thousand victories and defeats in the war which is fought daily and hourly in the human mind and soul: the war in the overcoming of self. Dissected and examined in detail this is a most unglamorous battle and to the outsider seems absurd; but it is the constant denying of the natural human urge to stay in bed longer than necessary, to eat or drink more than is justifiable, to be intolerant of the stupid, and to accumulate more than a fair share of this world's goods, that makes possible the gradual freeing of the human spirit.

—**SHEILA CASSIDY**, *Audacity to Believe*

TEN

Dancing for the World

FROM A YOUNG AGE, Zaida Catalán wanted to change the world. "As a 6-year-old girl I was devastated to see how human-kind was raping the Earth, through environmental pollution, and violating the sacred principles of life, of human beings and animals," the Swedish woman wrote in English in an autobi-ographical essay titled "Dancing for Myself."

"So I asked my mother, what kind of job could I have as an adult to change the world? Out of all the different profes-sions she mentioned, I knew I wanted to study law. As a girl I thought it seemed respectful and powerful enough to act as a platform to help put an end to the injustice in the world."

Like her mother, Maria Moresby, Zaida was already a veg-etarian and starting to defend it to others because of how it protected the animals of the world she loved. She loved reading. And she loved dancing. Alone in her room, she would turn up her music and dance by herself.

Zaida's father Mario had been arrested and tortured by the Pinochet regime in 1970s Chile. He escaped to Romania and then to Sweden, where he met Maria at a party and fell in love.

In rural Sweden, coming from an ethnically mixed vegetarian family didn't result in broad acceptance and friends for young Zaida. She was bullied at school. Yet she could somehow see far enough ahead to not become discouraged. "I knew I was going somewhere. I had a feeling in my stomach that told me so," she wrote in her essay.

She consumed books the way some children do candy. And she kept dancing.

She headed to law school at Stockholm University, living in a small apartment with her cat and still feeling alone. She wore her "hippie dress" to class and didn't fit in with her classmates who came from wealthier backgrounds. But she was active in the Green Party of Sweden and became a leader of its Youth Association in 2001, even becoming its spokesperson. That led to more opportunities, including working as a legal advisor in the party's office at the Parliament of Sweden. She helped the party work on issues such as gender equality and sexual violence, and helped craft policy. She went to Guatemala to help train young people on democracy and equality, and not only volunteered at a shelter to help women who experienced domestic abuse but joined national efforts to help women and children.

Zaida got her law degree in 2005, mourning that her father Mario was not there to see it. She cried because of the sacrifices he had made and because one of her greatest sources of motivation had been to make him proud. Though her relationship with her father grew strained as she got older, she felt his loss when he died in 2002 after an accident as he worked to renovate a property.

She was a rising star in the Green Party. In 2008, Zaida declared her candidacy for a seat in the European Parliament.

She was just twenty-eight. When a journalist asked what she hoped to achieve if elected, she laughed and said, "What don't I want to achieve?" She wanted to help make the laws for not just Sweden, but the entire EU. She wanted to fight for the climate and green jobs. She wanted to end the sex trade industry across Europe.

In the 2009 election, she earned sixteen thousand votes, but her upstart campaign ended in defeat, though she had earned the attention of many over the past dozen years with the Green Party. Journalists such as Staffan Lindberg, the *Aftonbladet* newspaper reporter who wrote a book on her titled *Mordet på Zaida Catalán* (*The murder of Zaida Catalán*), noted that journalists were often drawn to her youth and energy.[1]

But then she seemed to disappear from the public eye.

After the election loss in 2009, she extracted herself from politics because it became too slow for her as a way to enact change. "She was looking for ways to get out in the world and do real work, hands on," her friend Fredrik Krohnman said. She went from what she called committing "soul-suicide" to again finding the "fire of life" as she traveled the world.

In 2010, she became part of the Folke Bernadotte Academy, the Swedish government agency for peace, security, and development. She learned about protection against risks and threats in conflict areas and in January 2011 went to the DRC as an expert on gender, sexual violence, and human rights for the European Union Police Mission, known as EUPOL. She worked in Goma training police about sexual violence and gender-based violence with the goals of helping officers better understand how to help victims and empowering female officers. In one session, an officer challenged her, asserting that following her advice would lead to them being viewed as weak men. The Goma police chief David Bodeli stood and spoke, saying the man was wrong and that they had a responsibility to defend human rights. Zaida and David became friends that day.

After eighteen months in Goma, Zaida returned to Sweden and delivered a lecture at the Folke Bernadotte Academy titled "Dealing with Resistance When Working on Gender."

In 2013, Zaida went to Kabul, Afghanistan, with EUPOL on a similar assignment. She organized vegetarian meals and yoga classes for colleagues and vaccinated feral cats. She wrote in her diary, "I believe that a selfless act brings us closer to our hearts."

One day as she was lecturing, a month before she was to return to Sweden, a man with a bomb under his clothing entered the room next to her at a Kabul police station. The blast killed him and several others. She wasn't physically injured, but was shaken. "I knelt before the divine for giving me a chance to live again," she wrote, saying that she felt she'd gotten a second chance at life and a better understanding of what people experience living in war zones.

She kept working for justice. In 2015 and 2016, she took on another assignment for EUPOL in Ramallah, Palestine, as a gender expert. Her work first in Goma and then the Middle East led to her 2016 appointment on the Group of Experts alongside MJ. In her "Dancing with Myself" essay, she wrote, "When I set foot at the International Airport of Kinshasa I was sweating profusely. I was alone in one of the most lawless countries in the world and I had no idea of what I was getting myself into. But I knew I was in the right place. The heavy humid air, mixed with red earth and diesel fumes and chlorophyll, I knew I had arrived in [a] place where the heart resides." As it had for MJ and others, the Congo had captured her heart.

She said that despite the pain, despite the violence, the Congolese people fought for justice and better lives. "And they dance," she wrote. "They dance to smile, to sweat and to shake off the devil's grip."

Over Christmas 2016, MJ's mother's family had again gathered in northern Indiana. The Miller aunts, uncles, and cousins come together once a year at a bed and breakfast or somewhere where they can be a family in one place. MJ made it a priority to be at the gathering, even when he was working overseas.

The food the family enjoyed included cooked brisket and butterhorn rolls, pumpkin whoopee pies, and a salty party mix. Games stayed out on the table, and the young children received near-constant attention from the adults.

During these gatherings, the tradition is for the adults to tell "dummies" stories. They take turns sharing embarrassing moments. Overseas work provides many humbling experiences, and MJ was happy to share with the family about several of them.

The stories don't have to be new. Sometimes they're even reprised year over year, but the laughter is just as loud and hearty. That year, MJ told the story of the roosters and Patrick Maxwell's arrival in the DRC. The family howled as MJ described how he told Patrick the morning after the incident, "This place is crazy. I used to be the calmest person I know."

But he also told his family of visiting a prison to conduct interviews with people who had been captured. Over the course of a week, MJ was repeatedly asked for money by the officials who had joined him in the remote area. He interviewed the prisoners, who were starving, about the armed groups they had been part of. "It was just terrible," he said.

He barely managed to get on the plane that came just once a week, and then his luggage was stolen. MJ had run out of money and patience and was yelling at people, including members of the Republican Guard. Military intelligence returned the bag to him in Goma, but it was stolen again, and the adventure, as well as MJ's anger, continued. Though he loved the DRC, his life and work there was taking its toll on him.

During that visit to Indiana in late 2016, MJ also met with friends and told them of his work in the DRC. Over drinks at a bar in Goshen, MJ talked about his safety with Tim Nafziger, a Mennonite peace activist close to MJ's age. MJ told him that someone working for the UN was safer than others. He also spoke of how tired he was of bureaucracy, of filling out reports, and he made the offhand comment, "I didn't make plans beyond this, because I didn't think I'd live this long." Tim heard it as MJ saying that as he lived fully in the moment, he wasn't sure what his next plans were.

ℕ ℕ ℕ ℕ

That Christmas season, Zaida was in Kalmar with her mother and sister, but she was more stressed and edgy than usual. She spent hours in her room, writing on her computer.

Her sister Elizabeth heard her talking to a friend, acknowledging that her life had been threatened in the DRC. She had been interviewing a militia leader in a remote village when she overheard a comment that indicated that she could be killed. She and the UN office staff member who was translating left as quickly as they could.

Her sister challenged her about the danger of the work. Zaida said it was because Kabila's government wanted chaos to control people and postpone the election. She said that they had good protection and she was addressing the issue. "I cannot let fear rule," she told her sister.[2]

Zaida was, like the other experts, working on a variety of investigations.

Rape is a common weapon of war in the DRC. The most rigorous scientific study, published in 2011 by the *American Journal of Public Health*, counted that 1.69 million to 1.8 million Congolese women had been raped in their lifetime.[3] The numbers gathered in 2006 and 2007 were significantly higher than previous studies and cited that forty-eight women were raped every hour in the DRC and that more than four hundred thousand had been raped in the previous year. The highest numbers were in eastern DRC. In North Kivu, an average of sixty-seven women out of every thousand had been raped at least once.

In the poor village of Kavumu, in South Kivu, soldiers of Jeshi la Yesu (Army of Jesus) kidnapped a girl from her bed, raped her, and returned her or left her in a nearby field. Denis Mukwege, a Congolese physician and Nobel Peace Prize laureate, did extensive surgery on dozens of girls between 2013 and 2016 at Panzi Hospital in Bukavu after they had been raped by soldiers. The soldiers believed that "virgin blood" would protect them from bullets as they went into battle.

This is where Zaida's expertise and zeal came together. "She wanted to empower women first and foremost. She thought that could create change," said her sister Elizabeth. Zaida was

Zaida and MJ take a selfie together during UN meetings in New York City.
PHOTO USED BY PERMISSION OF MORESBY FAMILY

following the long Swedish tradition of going into the world to help others. The Scandinavian country prioritizes a benevolent approach, and its citizens tend to view the world with less nationalism than many others do. "We have two hundred years of peace. That does something with a people and a nation. We can afford to care about [other] countries, in a way," explained Zaida's friend Fredrik Krohnman.

Journalist Lauren Wolfe had published her first story about the rapes in April 2015, and Zaida read another by Wolfe in *The Guardian* in August 2016 the day before she left for the DRC. Wolfe's investigative journalism uncovered the organized attacks and tracked how the Congolese government had committed to investigating but hadn't taken action. Zaida then led an investigation of Frédéric Batumike Rugimbanja, the leader of the Army of Jesus group and a member of the South Kivu provincial assembly. Zaida realized that her friend David Bodeli was also investigating.

The Group of Experts report published in August 2017 established that Panzi Hospital had treated forty-two girls and stated, "Two militiamen and other sources told the Group that Jeshi la Yesu perpetrated child rapes as part of a ritual believed to render their combatants impervious to bullets. The militiamen also confirmed their group's rituals were led by a person called 'Kabuchungu' or 'Kabotchonga.' In June 2016, this person, together with Batumike and several members of the militia, were arrested on charges including rape of children and young girls."[4] In addition, Batumike and his men had likely killed some of his critics and threatened others.

The rapes in Kavumu ended after Batumike's arrest in June 2016. The powerful politician, who was a member of a party that was part of Kabila's coalition, would finally face justice, but there was evidence that Batumike had people protecting him and honoring his claim of immunity because of his role in the local parliament.

In late November 2017, Batumike and nine other men in Jeshi la Yesu went on trial for crimes against humanity for the horrific sexual violence. Two others were accused of being part of an armed group. A mobile court in eastern DRC conducted the trial and found the men guilty, sentencing them to life in prison. Justice from a court is rare in the DRC. The case was lauded as a landmark. In a *Guardian* story on the trial, Karen Naimer of Physicians for Human Rights said, "It's unprecedented, for who Batumike was: a very powerful provincial MP, with his group and his financial control. And the collaboration between civil society, doctors and the police will hopefully set precedents."[5]

It was the kind of victory that Zaida, who was killed eight months earlier, would have celebrated. It would have brought her great joy that a perpetrator had been held accountable for horrific crimes.

In her diary in late January 2017, she had written, "Exciting development. I can maybe nail this bastard. Damn!"

Had she meant Batumike? Or someone else?

ℼ ℼ ℼ ℼ

On March 2, ten days before Zaida and MJ disappeared, Zaida texted her friend Fredrik to say that she was going to a restaurant with a Congolese source and wanted to make sure someone knew.

Fredrik responded, "You know how mad I will be with you if you die."

On March 10, she asked David Bodeli for protection, saying he was the only police officer she trusted.

On Saturday, March 11, Zaida and Fredrik talked by phone for about an hour. As they talked about seeing one another again, they discussed the last time they had dinner at his place. "See you soon," he said.

"I hope fate will let us," she said.

He thought the response was odd. "That's not her. She didn't express herself that way," he said.

She knew they were on to something big, he said.

"They knew."

₪ ₪ ₪ ₪

In the summer of 2016, MJ was ready to call somewhere home.

Starting when he was in Germany, he would often visit Andy Gingerich, who was working in Albuquerque, New Mexico.

One night during one of these visits, MJ filled in for Andy on the softball field, pitching for his injured friend. As Andy looked out at him from the bench, MJ seemed comfortable, as if he belonged.

Andy had built a small guesthouse in the backyard of the Plex, a property with a house broken up into three units and several other small residences, including the one Andy built in the backyard.

The Plex is a place for young adults to live together, though they don't necessarily share resources in the same way the Hausgemeinschaft or other group houses sometimes do.

As MJ visited that summer, he went bowling with those who lived there and made plans to move there for good. In October, between trips to the DRC to do his UN work, he unpacked his tidy collection of belongings at the Plex. He shared a bathroom across the hall with housemates, including Anna Horner, who was a bit surprised the first time he burst in while she was brushing her teeth.

He told the others at the Plex that he had lived out of a suitcase for two years and was ready to settle in somewhere. Anna Horner said, "He was so enthusiastic about having chosen a place to drop roots and was ready to build relationship with just about anybody he crossed paths in that new location. In doing that, he strengthened a group of people who were neighbors into a deeper sense of community."

Anna had been trying for days to recruit others to help her pick chokecherries. MJ quickly agreed, and with Andy, the three headed out for a morning of picking berries. It was a magical morning, and Anna made jam from the berries and saved it for when MJ was to return from the DRC in mid-March.

The new friends at the Plex learned more about his UN work than other friends had. He showed them the photos of evidence that he had on his phone amid his personal photos. One day at a coffee shop, as Anna worked on a grant report for her more conventional job, MJ was at work on his computer and grew excited because he had identified someone in the DRC. Using social media and text messages, he had made a discovery helpful to his investigation. "He was showing me how he used his investigative skills to piece all this together," she said.

One night, as he watched the documentary *Virunga* about the mountain gorillas of eastern DRC, he kept stopping the movie and giving his own commentary. "He wanted us to get it and understand this world he was living in," said Amanda Clouse, who had become a good friend after at first being turned off by MJ. Her first encounter with him was hearing him tell a sexist joke: "What do you call a pretty woman at a Mennonite church? A visitor." She'd thought, "Oh, you're that guy," but later she was charmed by him.

Amanda said she saw MJ wanting to settle down and that he even had "baby fever."

He was trying to figure out what was next. He talked about being a paramedic or a marine biologist. He mentioned the prospect of going to an Ivy League school for a graduate program, but decided that he wouldn't be happy doing that. He also talked-ed about moving to Los Angeles with the woman he had started dating. He was musing about what his next adventure could be.

ℕ ℕ ℕ ℕ

MJ had ordered smart outlets and was tracking the shipment online.

The tracker showed that the package had been delivered to the Plex, and in an era before video doorbells made it easy to track so-called porch pirates, MJ couldn't understand where it was. "He was bringing it up to everybody," said Louis Wilcox, who was living there at the time.

The box had mistakenly been delivered to another unit of the Plex, and a housemate wanted to send MJ on a scavenger hunt. Together, the Plex residents and friends emptied the box of the purchase and replaced it with a rock and playful note. MJ would have to find his way from clue to clue.

One of the clues was revealed to him at the nearby coffee shop after he ordered a "gummy bear latte."

The housemates delighted in creating the clues and sending MJ on a playful mission. MJ was thrilled to undertake it and then to crack the code.

"He was giddy," said Louis.

In the end, he got the contents of the original package and a second shipment from the retailer, which replaced the first one after MJ contacted the company about the missing box.

He plugged some of the lamps of the house into the newly purchased outlets. Soon, when he was back in the Congo, the lights would flicker or dim. MJ was using his own technology on the other side of the world to playfully interact with the place he was wanting to call home.

He was less successful trying to crack the lock on Andrew and Amanda Clouse's front door across the street from the Plex. Andrew got locked out, and MJ tried to help him get in with his trusty lockpicking set.

He worked at it and told those watching, "You can't break a lock doing this. It's fine."

He was embarrassed that he and Andrew had to buy a new lock. While they were out buying it, Amanda texted to ask why she couldn't get in the front door after she arrived home. The new lock was installed quickly.

He had been so enthusiastic about using his longtime skill and then embarrassed when it didn't work. He was enthusiastic much of the time he was at the Plex, pouring energy into relationships as he became part of the community.

After moving to Albuquerque that fall, MJ went to a gym three or four days a week to do Brazilian jujitsu, a martial art that he had taken up in the past few years. As his friend Justin Ramer joked, for a pacifist he seemed to really enjoy beating people up. Anna saw it as self-care, a way he could deal with the trauma he'd seen and the stress he felt from the UN job.

He was also seeing a therapist to help process those things. The sessions incorporated eye movement desensitization and reprocessing (EMDR), a method that helps individuals work through traumatic experiences. He was worn down by the horrible things he was seeing in the Congo—and frustrated by the bureaucracy of the UN.

Yet at the Plex, MJ was full of life. He wasn't hedging a bet. He was all in. "He was so energetic when he was here," said Steve Miller, a longtime resident of the Plex. "He was here one hundred percent."

As he prepared to return to the DRC, MJ cooked the residents a big meal, including making a special portion of rice for someone who ate a gluten-free diet. He served as the disc jockey for a dance party.

Then a housemate took him to the airport as he headed to the DRC for what would be the last time.

What we would like to do is change the world—make it a little simpler for people to feed, clothe, and shelter themselves as God intended them to do. And, by fighting for better conditions, by crying out unceasingly for the rights of the workers, the poor, of the destitute—the rights of the worthy and the unworthy poor, in other words—we can, to a certain extent, change the world; we can work for the oasis, the little cell of joy and peace in a harried world. We can throw our pebble in the pond and be confident that its ever widening circle will reach around the world. We repeat, there is nothing we can do but love, and, dear God, please enlarge our hearts to love each other, to love our neighbor, to love our enemy as our friend.

—**DOROTHY DAY**, "Love Is the Measure," *The Catholic Worker*, June 1946

ELEVEN

In the Face of Evil

AS COORDINATOR OF the Group of Experts, MJ played a larger role in relating to UN officials, both when they visited the DRC and in New York.

On the last day of July 2016, a high-level delegation, which included UN staff and Security Council members from around the world, arrived in central Africa and spent a week traveling around the DRC, Rwanda, and Uganda. As coordinator, MJ helped plan the logistics, assured that background papers and talking points were in order, and served as a guide for the group. The group met with government officials around the Great Lakes region and in Kinshasa, discussing the issues outlined in the Group of Experts reports.

In mid-December 2016, MJ presented the midterm report to the UN Security Council in New York. He arrived early, wore a nice suit, read a prepared statement, and spent an extended time answering questions from the Security Council members. He was young, impressive, and stood out. Julie

Jolles, a political advisor for the US Mission to the UN in the State Department, remembers hearing MJ present the midterm report and participating in a meeting in the classified section of the US Mission to the UN. After the intense hour-long meeting, he followed her into her office to talk more about the DRC. "He was just really memorable," she said. "He was very present. Mostly because he was so eager and so ready to discuss details."

Nowhere in the 2016 midterm report does it mention an increasingly dangerous situation in Kasai-Central, a province in the center of the DRC. It doesn't receive mention in the mandate or the individual research plans for any of the Group of Experts, but a number of people in the diplomatic community were growing alarmed.

Horrible reports and even videos were starting to surface from the region, and officials were starting to worry that President Kabila's desire to hold on to power was causing instability to spread to the Kasais. The province of Kasai-Central is a center for gold and diamond mining, yet is one of the poorest provinces in the DRC.

Instability seemed to be spreading fast in the provinces, and officials in New York were focused on other areas and other problems in the DRC. Historically, the Kasais were explored and investigated far less than the Kivus, and while attention in New York had grown as election delays continued, the Kasais were not getting the attention they deserved as a new armed group emerged.

The Kamuina Nsapu is a clan of people composed of the Luba ethnic group, indigenous to central Congo and centered in several villages about forty miles southeast of Kananga. Jean-Pierre Mpandi became the leader in 2011, but his appointment wasn't recognized by provincial and national government officials as is usually common practice in the DRC. The government recognition was important and political, as traditional chiefs receive salaries and manage villages.

Kabila is unpopular in the region, and the Kamuina Nsapu are opposed to institutions, including churches, schools, and the government. Yet Mpandi took offense that the government wouldn't recognize him. In April 2016, when he was in South Africa, provincial authorities sent security forces to raid his home. He incited his followers to rise up against the government forces, calling them foreign mercenaries and an occupying force.

Some of his soldiers were children as young as five years old who had been drugged and armed with spears or machetes before being sent into combat.

On August 12, 2016, Mpandi and some of his men were killed by Congolese security forces. Videos filmed by soldiers who said they belonged to the Congolese army showed the attacks, including the killing of ten children armed with sticks. Mpandi's body was taken, denying the group its traditional burial. Photos of his dead body released over the following months added to the outrage among the Kamuina Nsapu.

They continued to attack the security forces near Kananga, and there were deaths on both sides. A UNICEF document from early September 2016, as quoted by journalist Sonia Rolley, counted fifty-one dead, twenty-one settlements affected by the conflict, 806 burned buildings, and nearly twelve thousand people displaced.[1]

The Kamuina Nsapu kept attacking, including the Kananga airport. The clashes continued between the militia and government forces. Refugees were flooding out of the region, churches and schools were being destroyed, the death toll was mounting, and mass graves were being used to bury the dead.

Recognizing the increasing risk that violence in the Kasais would spread even further and hoping to ensure that high-level officials in New York and Goma who had the authority to direct MONUSCO would take action, MJ and Zaida headed to Kananga to investigate in late January 2017, a month after MJ presented the midterm report to the UN Security Council and a few weeks after he returned to the DRC.

On January 31, MJ and Zaida interviewed a ranking official of the General Assembly in Kananga who claimed that the government was trying to negotiate with the Kamuina Nsapu. Prime Minister Samy Badibanga had been planning to visit the region but had canceled a few days earlier. That same day, the Kamuina Nsapu kidnapped a Catholic priest, who was later released.

On February 1, MJ and Zaida interviewed a UNICEF official in the city who had worked in the area for nearly a dozen years and told them the poverty of the area and the politics were both contributing to the conflict.

Over the next two weeks, additional battles between the Kamuina Nsapu and FARDC resulted in more dead. The confirmed numbers varied, but the UN reported more than one hundred deaths from February 9 to 13, including thirty-nine women killed in a market by security forces targeting the Kamuina Nsapu.

MONUSCO accused the army of using rocket launchers in the battles—against militiamen carrying wooden weapons. On February 17, a leaked video on social media showed security forces executing Kamuina Nsapu members. Government officials claimed that the video could not be verified or that it had been taken in another country. The images of soldiers firing at unarmed victims on the ground, bleeding, sent shock waves through the international community.

On February 20 in Geneva, Zeid Ra'ad Al Hussein, the UN High Commissioner for Human Rights, issued a statement calling for a halt to the killings. "There are multiple, credible allegations of massive human rights violations in Kasai, Kasai Central, Kasai Oriental and Lomami provinces, amid a sharp deterioration in [the] security situation there, including people being targeted by soldiers for their alleged affiliation with a local militia," said Zeid. "It is time to stop a blunt military response that does nothing to tackle the root causes of the conflict between the Government and local militias but instead targets civilians on the basis of their presumed links to the militias."[2]

The release also said, "The UN peacekeeping mission, MONUSCO, is not in a position to verify the origin and authenticity of the video. However, the DRC Government spokesperson and Minister of Communication Lambert Mende has stated that FARDC officers are under judicial investigation for their behavior during recent fighting in the village."

The February progress update for the Group of Experts, likely written using MJ and Zaida's research, stated, "Shooting by security services led to civilian deaths." It also said the group was continuing to investigate both the use of child soldiers by Kamuina Nsapu and the use of excessive force by the Congolese army and police.

Members of the Group of Experts discussed whether the Kamuina Nsapu were actually an armed group, with at least one member advocating that they weren't, though what was happening there could be relevant for Zaida because of the humanitarian issue.

As reports of the violence spread, as more videos showed horror, the pressure mounted to find out what was going on in Kasai-Central.

אַ אַ אַ אַ

The whole time MJ had been in the DRC, he had been going into the bush to talk to warlords.

He preferred motorcycles to the Land Cruisers often used by expats and diplomats. He relished going to someone rather than staying in an office. His safety often depended on the people he was with. When he worked for MCC, he gained some level of protection by saying he worked for the church, which is generally revered in the DRC.

He continued to rely on Moise and Emmanuel to help him with his work and trusted their counsel and experience. The insight and trust they'd developed working together over several years offered him some protection as he did inherently risky work.

Investigating armed groups in a country where so many have died over hundreds of years is dangerous work, yet MJ would tell friends and family that he was at more risk when traveling in the Middle East. Being part of the UN, which has its own drones and special forces, offers some inherent protection.

Many who do the work have a story about a close call. Bally Mutumayi, who worked in the UN office in Goma, was traveling with a member of the Group of Experts several years before MJ was hired. Bally and the expert were in the bush and were apprehended by the Mai Mai militia. The men were released after being held overnight. They were in an area with no ability to connect by telephone. The militia contacted the commander whom the UN workers were intending to visit and released them after the commander affirmed that he was expecting them.

Foreigners have rarely been targeted in the DRC, though when it does happen it makes international news. The experts, men and women, went into the field to get information and came back to tell about it. If you stay in the big cities or towns to do the work, you don't get the job done, said Jason Stearns, who coordinated the Group of Experts in 2008 and has worked extensively in the DRC.

Members of the Group of Experts did security assessments and then often went into the field. "That's our job to a certain extent," said Jason. They often used motorcycles, which are cheaper and easier to use on bad roads.

"What happened to Michael could have happened to me," said Jason, voicing a comment a number of others said about their work in the DRC.

The UN didn't ask how the experts got their information. Over the years, some were reckless in how they approached the work, according to Dan Fahey, a former Group of Experts member. "I saw people acting in ways that put themselves at risk and the national staff at risk," he said.

Emilie Serralta, another former group coordinator, discussed with MJ the tension of delivering good reports with "sexy investigative finds." The pressure didn't come from the UN, but from the others on a team who wanted to make the DRC a better place and who sometimes connected their ego to their ability to make those finds.

Most of the experts were mindful of alerting others to their plans and not traveling alone. MJ was fastidious about those things and often did more.

Dan had requested devices that could help track someone and even signal for help. He saw a former British military soldier with one and saw how he could track someone in real time on a computer. He asked the UN office in New York and was told there wasn't money to purchase them.

Experts occasionally used such equipment of their own accord, but not universally. MJ bought a Garmin Fēnix 3 watch that had tracking ability. He would sometimes turn it on and share the link with family or friends so they could see him moving around the DRC. They saw it as one more gadget, something he loved. But since he also bought one for one of his colleagues, it's likely that he saw it as a way to mitigate risk, just as he encrypted his computer data in a way that made it nearly impossible to crack.

When Jason Stearns was with the UN, he used an email address from Yahoo to contact governments he was investigating and didn't have access to encrypted phones. By the time MJ was doing the work, he could at least use WhatsApp, which is encrypted from end to end, as well as UN email. He did all he could to assure his own safety and the safety of those around him.

₪ ₪ ₪ ₪

On Monday, March 5, 2017, MJ had a nice meal and a few beers with Christoph Vogel at a restaurant in Goma. The two had become close friends. As the two experts on armed groups, they did nearly all their investigations together, except the one in Kasai where MJ and Zaida were working together. The two men had been together on a mission in the east and had a rare evening where both of them were in the same place with nothing on the schedule.

MJ told his friend about his pranks of the past. "I was utterly impressed," Christoph said. "I had been doing a lot of big pranks in high school but I had definitely found my master. That was so amazing."

It was the kind of conversation that wasn't just about their work and investigations. They could relax for a bit and talk about things other than their tasks. When they were in the DRC doing their UN work, they would usually call twice a day, in the morning and evening, to update each other.

On Wednesday, March 8, MJ and Zaida landed in Kananga aboard a UN plane arranged by Bally Mutumayi. MJ had walked into the Goma UN office and told him, "Bally, I need you. We have a trip. We are going to Kasai." Usually Bally or one of the other drivers/translators would go along on such a trip, but none of them could speak the languages of the region, including Tshiluba. Another group member said he needed Bally in Bukavu, so Bally made the travel arrangements and took Zaida and MJ to the Goma airport to fly first to Kinshasa and then to Kananga.

MJ and Zaida started meeting with individuals in Kananga. As in other investigations, they were collecting information from officials but were also working to find and interview eye-witnesses of the violence between the government soldiers and the Kamuina Nsapu. Staying in Kananga and talking to official sources wasn't enough. They wanted the names of the Kamuina Nsapu members putting children in harm's way and the government officers ordering the violence. In a battle between the government and a rebel group, the quest for truth wasn't clear-cut.

They arranged a meeting with Col. Jean de Dieu Mambweni, who offered to help them. The military officer put them in touch with Betu Tshinsela as a local interpreter and fixer, who then stayed in touch with the colonel every time he spoke with Zaida.

Over the next two days, MJ and Zaida made plans to go visit the Kamuina Nsapu near Bunkonde in the southern part of the province.

Betu Tshinsela helped arrange a meeting at a hotel, where they gathered in a room with representatives of the Kamuina Nsapu, including an elder with the group named Francois Muamba. Other men, in addition to Betu Tshinsela, were there. José Tshibuabua, a relative of Betu, was likely there, and was later shown to be on the payroll of Agence national de renseignement (ANR), the national intelligence agency for the DRC.

MJ and Zaida had been investigating a number of men in the Kamuina Nsapu and told a former Group of Experts member in February that the leader who replaced Mpandi, a man named Jacques Kabeya, may have been co-opted by the ANR.

Zaida was trying to map the relationships between these men and whether they were involved with a government minister named Clément Kanku. Though Kanku worked for the government, Zaida believed he was involved in the burning of a village. She had a recording of him celebrating that the Kamuina Nsapu had burned down a government building in August 2016.

Zaida secretly recorded the March 11 meeting at the hotel. That recording later became a key in understanding how MJ and Zaida found themselves in danger.

ן ן ן ן

Eight people gathered around the table at the Wood Land Guest House. Bottles of beer were on the table in front of them, part of the formality of a meeting such as this.

MJ introduced himself and Zaida in French and explained that they worked for the UN Security Council and went out to gather information. They asked for assurances of their safety and were told that they could go safely to Bunkonde.

Their question was translated to Francois Muamba, and he responded in the language of Tshiluba, "You do not know what happens there, believe me," he said to the interpreters. "Do not give guarantees. They will be attacked."

The interpreters encouraged MJ and Zaida to go.

"You can go there with no problems," they were told.

ן ן ן ן

The next morning, MJ was frustrated with not being able to leave on time. He told French journalist Sonia Rolley, who was also working nearby, that they were going south for the day to meet some of the groups. "Should be back before late to catch up."

That morning, MJ and Christoph, in the eastern part of the country, couldn't talk by phone, but exchanged texts. "We wished each other a safe trip," Christoph said. Even that morning, as he waited to leave the hotel, MJ texted Steve Miller at the Plex about how he would survive the trip. He was hoping it would be his last trip in this role and that he could soon do something different.

MJ and Zaida finally left on the back of motorcycles late morning with Betu Tshinsela and three drivers. They likely had to go through army and military checkpoints where MJ or one of the people accompanying them explained what they were doing and allowed to pass—something he would have done hundreds of times over his years in the DRC.

An aid worker saw them in the middle of the day, but what filled their afternoon still isn't clearly known. Late that afternoon, Elizabeth Moresby's phone rang in Sweden with a call from her sister Zaida's cell phone. And then they were missing.

Within hours, the UN had instituted a security protocol. Christoph and others hadn't heard from them. Around ten that night, when Christoph called Zaida's phone, someone answered but again didn't speak.

The search for the two missing UN experts began.

The news that MJ was missing sparked prayer and deep concern among his family and friends. Yet so many of them believed that MJ could talk his way out of this as he had so many times before.

They believed if anyone could talk their way out of it, it was MJ. That's what he did. That's who he was.

₪ ₪ ₪ ₪

The day MJ and Zaida went missing—March 12, 2017—is also the day we now know they were killed.

It was the second anniversary of MJ's joining the UN Group of Experts.

It was also a marker in a killing spree that got the attention of US diplomats.

The Office of the UN High Commissioner for Human Rights (OHCHR) confirmed that 251 people, including sixty-two children, were killed between March 12 and June 19 in Kasai-Central.

It was horrible.

A communication to the US State Department from the UN, which then became part of the State Department's *2017 Country Reports on Human Rights Practices: Democratic Republic of the Congo*, reported that "according to eyewitnesses, the Catholic Church, and UN personnel, civilians executed by the State-Security Forces included children as young as six months old, some of whom were shot in their beds."[3]

On March 14 and 15, the FARDC, called a "State-Security Force" by the UN, killed at least one hundred people in Kananga.

From March 28 to 30, the army reportedly killed hundreds more civilians using a tactic of cordoning off an area and searching for Kamuina Nsapu members.

The numbers were one thing. The fact that children were being brutalized is what eventually alarmed US diplomats. The country report stated:

The OHCHR reported that "local security forces and other officials actively fomented, fueled, and occasionally led, attacks on the basis of ethnicity." According to the OHCHR, "survivors have spoken of hearing the screams of people being burned alive, of seeing loved ones chased and cut down, of themselves fleeing in terror." The OHCHR also reported that the State Security Forces and local authorities supported and allegedly armed a militia, the Bana Mura, responsible for killing civilians in Kasai. According to the OHCHR, "FARDC soldiers were seen leading groups of Bana Mura militia during attacks on villages." In April and May, the Bana Mura reportedly attacked ethnic Luba and Lulua, "beheading, mutilating, and shooting victims; in some cases burning them alive in their homes." The OHCHR determined that, in one attack on April 24, in the village of Cinq, "90 patients, colleagues and people who had sought refuge in a health center were killed, including patients who could not escape when the surgical ward was set on fire." The OHCHR reported seeing "children as young as two whose limbs had been chopped off; many babies had machete wounds and severe burns. One two-month-old baby seen . . . had been hit by two bullets four hours after birth; the mother was also injured. At least two pregnant women were sliced open and their foetuses mutilated."[4]

The country's Council of Catholic Bishops estimated that the Congolese army killed 400 people in Kananga in March alone and that at least 3,383 civilians were killed in Kasai between October 2016 and June 19, 2017, by government forces or rebel militia groups.

The killing of the children didn't make international news. The accusations that the Kamuina Nsapu beheaded thirty-nine or forty police officers by the government did. A video posted to YouTube by police showed policemen sitting on the ground amid the alleged Kamuina Nsapu militia members.

The group likely beheaded several others, including the wife of a mayor and a National Independent Electoral Commission (CENI) official. Sonia Rolley noted that the group sees the state and its representatives as its enemies, because it operates a repressive regime. Churches and schools can be targeted for this reason. It's also the basis for why enemies can be decapitated after being accused and justification is found.

₪ ₪ ₪ ₪

John and Michele, in the face of terrifying news that their son was missing, had to make choices. They communicated privately with their daughters and their families, Andy Gingerich, Keith Grubaugh, and a few others in a private WhatsApp group.

They agreed to allow their phones to be tapped by US federal officials in case kidnappers called.

They also opted to be public about what they knew and were experiencing. Some organizations, such as MCC, would advise the family of someone who was missing to stay silent, to wait for news before speaking publicly.

John and Michele took a different path.

In the weeks when MJ was missing, as news coverage in Africa, Europe, and North America noted the disappearance, John, in particular, offered words on Facebook and received expressions of concern from people around the world, many of whom had been touched in some way by MJ's life.

In the DRC, Rachel Sweet, Timo Mueller, Christoph Vogel, and others worked their contacts to try to find out where MJ and Zaida were. Moise Butimbushi, who had worked alongside MJ at both MCC and the UN, traveled to Kasai-Central to try to find them. People around the world prayed as they waited for news.

MONUSCO, under the leadership of Col. Luis Mangini, searched for the two on the premise that they were still alive. On the night of Sunday, March 12, Col. Mangini received a call from a woman in an NGO who had worked with MJ and was worried about their disappearance that day. Around midnight, he got notice from MONUSCO headquarters that the two were missing.[5]

A company of 240 MONUSCO soldiers from Uruguay was in Kananga and started reconnaissance on Monday, March 13, with a helicopter, cars, and six armored personnel carriers. On Tuesday, Col. Mangini requested seventy

MONUSCO special forces soldiers from Tanzania and another helicopter from Ukraine to help with the mission. They arrived on Thursday.

The company commander in Kananga had met with MJ and Zaida before their intended trip to Bunkonde. They didn't ask for an escort and didn't want one when the commander offered, according to Col. Mangini.

NGOs that knew MJ assisted with information, and the special forces and Uruguayan company began searching and creating a map of the jungle as they did so. "Nobody was saying they were dead. For this reason, I named the operation, 'Rescue,'" Col. Mangini said.

With two interpreters who spoke Tshiluba, one of the local languages, they asked people what happened. One said he witnessed the ambush on March 12, and then he ran away. Col. Mangini asked for help from the Congolese army and local police. Not only did they not help, but they tried to block movements and take over patrols and aircraft.

The MONUSCO soldiers walked in the jungle with shovels, finding bodies buried in shallow graves, but not those of MJ and Zaida.

A helicopter crew spotted dirt that had been moved, and a patrol of around thirty Uruguayan soldiers dug up the spot. They found two bodies, buried side by side about two and a half feet deep. The head of one of the bodies was missing.

"The patrol called me, and I joined them there," said Col. Mangini. "I confirmed they were their bodies—I felt so sad."

A helicopter took the bodies to Kananga, where they were cleaned, and the soldiers kept searching for Zaida's head. It has never been found.

An autopsy was conducted in the DRC and then another in Kampala, Uganda, attended by officials from MONUSCO and the US State Department and an FBI agent. Because an

American citizen was reported as kidnapped in a foreign country, the FBI was involved early on and well after the deaths.

MJ's cause of death was determined to be a gunshot wound to the head. Zaida also died from a gunshot.

On March 27, when John and Michele learned that it was most likely MJ and Zaida who had been found in the shallow grave, John posted to Facebook:

> Dear friends,
>
> This is a message I hoped never to write. We have been informed that two Caucasian bodies have been found in shallow graves in the search area, one male and one female. Since no other Caucasians have been reported missing in that region, there is a high probability that these are the bodies of MJ and Zaida. Dental records and DNA samples will be used to confirm the identities. This will take some time.
>
> All other words fail me.

₪ ₪ ₪ ₪

John and Michele flew to New York City to meet their son's body.

It was not a happy homecoming, but they found ways to celebrate his life and spirit, to offer grace and healing to others, as they carried out what every parent hopes to avoid.

A UN staff member from the New York office made arrangements for John and Michele and others to receive the body and gather together.

Zobel Behalal, who was on the Group of Experts with MJ and Zaida, had traveled to Kampala to meet the body and then accompany it to Amsterdam and New York City. At their first meeting, Michele approached Zobel, smiled at him, and gave him a hug. He told her that it was difficult for him and said, "I'm so sorry." She told him that it wasn't his fault.

Other people from the UN who worked with MJ wanted to meet with John and Michele and express condolences. The New York office staff member found them a conference room in the basement of a hotel along the highway near the airport. What was expected to be a quick meeting ended up as seven hours of conversation around a long table. Michele wanted to hear how every one of them had interacted with MJ. An executive assistant told them, "Your son was so respectful of me. He never hung up the phone without thanking me."

The woman recounted how, as she had told MJ about one of the last trips she arranged for him, she expected him to protest the long layover, as others would have. "He said, 'That's fine. They know me there probably by name by now and I'll just work.'" Then he had added, "Sandra, I hope you know how much we appreciate all you do for us.'" The woman said it meant the world to her how he treated those who worked in support roles.

As they ordered and ate lunch, the staffers and parents kept talking. They didn't offer platitudes or hollow assurances. Michele made sure they knew that MJ's mission in the DRC was to "help people in violent situations be reconciled and work at peaceful solutions. He worked at that."

When someone asked John and Michele what justice they wanted, John said, "I don't know what justice looks like in this case; we're not looking for legal justice, which increases the cycle of violence and does not make sense. What we hope for is shalom justice, where people get what they need, not what they deserve." He suggested that the perpetrators be sentenced to twenty years of walking through the forests unarmed to serve internally displaced people by carrying water and digging latrines.

After some time, Hasmik Egian, director of the Security Council Affairs Division, looked at her colleagues and said that they rarely talk about faith together and that it was amazing to do so.

Julie Jolles, the State Department employee who worked for US Ambassador to the United Nations Nikki Haley, watched John and Michele respond with and offer grace to those they encountered. As they came to meet their son's body, they were carrying their beliefs in peace and justice, embodying the teachings of Jesus. They graciously extended grace and peace to others they encountered. "That is the peace that comes with this and yet it offers no peace to them," Julie said.

One of the UN staffers told them how good it had been to be together, to have that conversation. Michele said these people were part of MJ's life, and they wanted to recognize that.

As they went to the airport, staff told John and Michele they couldn't go out to the tarmac to greet the casket, as families of soldiers often do. "That didn't matter to us," said Michele. "Pomp and circumstance wasn't about us."

In fact, they had asked that his casket not be draped with an American flag as a soldier's would have been. John was adamant about that. He wanted to downplay nationalism. If anything, it

John and Michele Sharp meet with US Ambassador to the United Nations Nikki Haley (*left*) in New York City after MJ Sharp's death. PHOTO FROM THE US MISSION TO THE UNITED NATIONS

should be the UN flag more befitting the work of an unarmed peacemaker working internationally.

In the hangar, John and Michele stood next to a steel box, with arrows pointing to the head and feet, spending a few moments before they rode with MJ's body to a funeral home.

His body was put into a wooden casket. "When we entered the funeral home chapel, there it was draped in a US flag, so I removed it," said John. He quickly took the flag off the closed casket. They had hoped to be able to view MJ's remains but were prohibited from doing so because of the decomposition.

John wrote on Facebook: "Because the 'dust-to-dust' process was so far along, we did not have the option of viewing what was left of his body yesterday. So, in a Dover, Delaware, funeral home we sat by a borrowed coffin containing MJ's remains. Here Michele had a healing mental conversation with MJ. Perhaps the bright sunshine softened our grief. But nothing tempered the autopsy report of MJ's violent death. My anger compounded my grief, and so I carry this in my wounded spirit." He wrote that since the exact date of death couldn't be determined, they were choosing March 15 because the ides of March seemed fitting. The memorial service would be April 15 in Hesston, Kansas.

Michele stood next to the coffin in the chapel and talked to her son about his life, about his commitment. She felt a peace when the conversation was done.

As they prepared to return to Kansas, John and Michele received a small metal box, wrapped in cloth with a bow on top, of MJ's cremated remains. UN staff went with them to Baltimore-Washington Airport and met with the head of security so that they could easily get on the plane.

As she settled into her seat, Michele put the box between her feet. After takeoff, she picked up the box and put it in her lap, holding the ashes of her son there during the flight home.

We are all going to die, and I suppose whether it is sooner or later makes little difference in eternity, for eternity is total is-ness, immediacy, now-ness. Living in eternity is, in fact, the way we are supposed to live all the time, right now, in the immediate moment, not hanging on to the past, not projecting into the future. The past is the rock that is under our feet, that enables us to push off from it and move into the future. But we don't go bury ourselves in the past, nor should we worry too much about the future.

—**MADELEINE L'ENGLE**, *Sold into Egypt*

TWELVE

Gathering on the Plains

ANDY GINGERICH LOWERED his tall, lean frame into the 2011 Volkswagen Golf TDI and started the diesel engine.

He eased the car into gear and, with his brother Josh in the passenger seat, pulled away from the curb outside his house in Albuquerque.

They were packed for a trip they'd often made with family members to Hesston, Kansas, a small farming town north of Wichita. The six hundred plus miles on I-40 and US 54, through northeast New Mexico, north Texas, the Oklahoma Panhandle, and southeast Kansas, were familiar.

Josh and Andy had lived in Hesston as boys. After a move to Albuquerque for a few years, they had ended up in Middlebury, Indiana, just down the street from Andy's future best friends MJ and Keith.

As he left Albuquerque on that day in April 2017, Andy was driving MJ's car. Behind Andy and Josh were most of MJ's earthly belongings, packed into boxes. As he drove, Andy remembered so many previous car trips with MJ, expecting the next adventure. But this drive was about grief, not expectation.

Friends at the Plex had gathered and packed their friend's clothes and gadgets. "It was easy to pack up into his car," Andy said. There wasn't a lot to pack. The physical task wasn't difficult, but given what had happened to MJ, how he had died, the emotion was.

"It was hard for a lot of people to be in the room and pack it up. It was heavy, but I felt like it was an honor to drive it back. Kind of like a pallbearer or something," Andy said.

Years of work first in Germany and then in the DRC had taught MJ to live lean, to be able to move easily. Even as he settled into a new place to live in Albuquerque in the fall of 2016, he hadn't brought much with him. When he left for the Democratic Republic of the Congo in January 2017 to do another investigation as the leader of the United Nations Group of Experts, he traveled light, carrying a few clothes and a laptop that held the results of five years of work in Congo.

Andy had talked with his friend about the work, about what it means to be young Anabaptist Mennonites. Their fathers worked in the Mennonite church and their mothers had chosen helping professions. They respected their parents and the work they did. MJ and Andy talked about the legacy their parents' generation would leave behind—more than they talked about their own legacy. They had years to talk about that. They were just trying to figure out what came next in their own work, their own relationships. They had time.

Until March 12, they thought they had time.

₪ ₪ ₪ ₪

Andy was at work in an Albuquerque city office when he got the news. His boss drove him to his parents' house, where Andy told them and his brother Josh. "I've never seen my dad cry like that," said Andy.

As news broke of the deaths, others wept and wondered, sometimes in groups and sometimes in solitude.

MJ had told family and friends that his work was dangerous, that investigating the roots of violence and those who conscripted child soldiers wasn't easy. "But he always talked about how it would be so stupid for somebody to target an American or somebody who works for the UN. That would be so stupid," his sister Erin recalled him saying. He had told her if he died it would be because he was in the wrong place at the wrong time, not because he was targeted.

In Congo's bloody history, millions of people have died violently. The violence often targets its own residents, starting with the massacre of more than ten million Congolese enacted by King Leopold II of Belgium during his reign from 1865 to 1909.

Photos of Zaida and MJ adorn a table at the front of the church at Zaida's memorial service in Kalmar, Sweden. PHOTO COURTESY JOHN SHARP

The death toll has only continued to mount in the DRC, with many of the victims uncounted and some people buried in mass graves. MJ, Zaida, and others worked to count the dead and name those responsible. Yet those deaths weren't as newsworthy outside of Congo as the deaths of MJ and Zaida, as MJ had predicted.

ᚒ ᚒ ᚒ ᚒ

Michael "MJ" Sharp had been an all-American boy who loved fishing and hunting, playing sports, and orchestrating games and pranks on the expectant and unsuspecting. He had traveled the world, demonstrating the way of peace his people had espoused for five hundred years. The gaping questions of who killed him and why were part of what people brought to the memorial service as they traveled to the small Kansas town of Hesston.

Some of those making the trek to Kansas had attended memorials in the DRC and Germany. In Albuquerque, Andy and others had gathered around a campfire at the Plex and eaten the chokecherry jam as part of the remembering.

From all over the world, people came to hear the stories, to find solace. On this Easter weekend, the stories of someone who seemed larger than life were resurrected.

MJ's family and closest friends had been in nearly constant contact for a month by the time they gathered. On Thursday, April 13, the one-month anniversary of their learning of his disappearance, Keith Grubaugh and the Sharp family gathered together over supper, finally dealing with their grief face-to-face.

Others who came were visiting Kansas for the first time, and some were making their inaugural visit to the United States. Keith drove a rented van between Hesston and Wichita multiple times, fetching those who were arriving. Friends in Hesston and Newton, a slightly larger city nearby, opened their homes to strangers. Colette and Ron Mininger lodged Emmanuel Billay and Moise Butimbushi across the street from the Sharps in the same subdivision. The two men were able to converse in French, as Colette is Congolese and Ron, an American, had worked in the country on mining projects. In the warm spring weather, with high temperatures in the seventies, the Congolese men shivered in the air conditioning. Some of MJ's extra clothes from his room in the basement of the Sharp house were brought over for the men to wear.

Mennonites coming from other communities found other Mennonites with spare beds. Others stayed in Wichita or at the AmericInn near the Sharp home, which became the gathering hub for the weekend.

Friends and neighbors organized food for those gathered. In addition to the traditional meal after the service at the church, the Sharps hosted four other meals but didn't cook or shop for any of them. Casseroles, cinnamon rolls, and coffee cakes showed up at their house from hands eager to help.

₪ ₪ ₪ ₪

On Saturday afternoon, people headed for Hesston Mennonite Church, a large structure along Main Street and on the edge of Hesston College, the two-year school at which John was then a history and Bible professor. People filed into the church and filled many of the pews. Friends with whom MJ had bowled and women he had dated sat alongside people with whom he had worked. Christoph Vogel and the others on MJ's team with the United Nations were there, as well as Dr. Moussa Ba, chief of the Critical Incident Stress Management Unit for the UN, and three FBI agents.

A number of the men wore dark suits like the one Michele went with MJ to buy when he got the United Nations job. He hated wearing it and often loosened his tie.

A photo of him in the suit, tie loosened, was on the front table in the sanctuary, along with one of Zaida. There were also four candles representing the others who traveled with them on the day they were killed. At the time, they were believed to be victims of the attack rather than part of a plot, but later the plot became more apparent and the men's whereabouts are still part of the mystery.

Once the family was seated, Molly Hostetter started playing piano. Erin's oldest daughter, then eighteen, had traveled from Chicago to her uncle's memorial service, the uncle she had never met. Erin had tried to make arrangements for her brother and daughter to meet, but it hadn't happened in time. When Erin asked whether she was sure about coming to the memorial service weekend, she told her, "I don't want to miss one more thing."

As Molly took her seat after playing, John and Michele climbed the steps to the stage and stood behind the podium. "Thank you for coming," John said. He welcomed those watching via the livestreamed video and thanked everyone for the support, for the prayers, and even for stepping in to teach his classes at Hesston College.

Michele told those gathered how they treasured the stories that people had shared during the ordeal. "He lived life with a lot of passion and vigor and that's how we remember him today. Thank you for sharing it with us," she said.

Family and friends went to the podium to play music, read his obituary, or offer reflections.

"Knowing MJ, he would think you're all going overboard with the praise and compliments," said Erin when she spoke. "He would appreciate me pointing out that he was a regular guy."

₪ ₪ ₪ ₪

Keith Grubaugh stood at the podium, flanked by his wife Jenna and Andy Gingerich, and told the group that MJ was the best friend he would ever have and was a foundational piece of his life.

Jenna had met MJ on the weekend she married Keith. At their wedding, MJ read 1 Corinthians 13, a text that describes what Christian love looks and acts like. They too became best friends, and she would push him on the "touchy-feely" stuff that made him uncomfortable. "MJ managed to show his love in so many ways other than words," she said. MJ had sat with Jenna's grandmother and entertained their three-year-old. He had humored Jenna, who had a minor in peace studies, as they talked about the topic he knew much more about, she said. "He cared about and respected Keith more than anybody I've ever met," she said as she wiped away tears. "He lived and died loving the world and left a legacy to continue."

Andy took his turn at the podium, and told how he met MJ when they were both middle schoolers at the Wichita 95 church convention. He recounted how a few months later, at Heritage Middle School, the divider between their two classrooms had opened and Andy had heard MJ say, "Sugar Boy?"

"MJ was adventurous, boundary-defying, overly intelligent, curious, prankster," said Andy, reflecting on the trio they became along with Keith. "Keith was an inside-out, say-what-he-thinks, hardworking, disciplined family man. Both were faster than me, more athletic, better at video games, more confident with women, and caught a lot more fish. I was just an aimless dude who loved to be along for the ride."

As adults their lives would separate and come together again. Andy moved to Albuquerque and MJ traveled the world. "I was working on home. He was working on the globe. I was his dude. And he was my hero. But what's a hero?" Andy said, echoing *The Big Lebowski*.

In the short time MJ had spent at the Plex with Andy in Albuquerque, he had built a connection so strong it felt like the neighborhood stood still when he was gone for good.

"I'm not here to mourn his legend, because his legend will continue on and his work will continue to speak to us," Andy said. "I'm here to mourn the loss of my friend. Not the man of the newspapers, but the boy I went fishing with. But then again, it's all mixed together."

Andy picked up his guitar and sang the song based on the Menno Simons text that the two of them sang in high school choir, prefacing it with how MJ's faith was defined by "giving himself to the world."

He strummed the guitar, more confident and at home than he had been while speaking. Though MJ wouldn't have been comfortable with the way evangelicalism is talked about in the United States in the early twenty-first century, Andy said, he would have touted Menno's view of it. "His faith was just giving himself to the world," Andy said before strumming his guitar and singing, "True evangelical faith cannot lie sleeping. For it clothes the naked, it comforts the sorrowful, it gives to the hungry food. And it shelters the destitute."

₪ ₪ ₪ ₪

MJ's coworkers at the memorial service touted his prowess and told what they learned from him as a friend.

"What I've marveled at is MJ really did grow into this expert. This global political analyst and respected and courageous peace worker," said David Stutzman, who had worked alongside MJ in the Military Counseling Network in Germany.

They won victories, getting approval for those soldiers seeking conscientious objector status. They laughed together. They were brothers in arms. "He came to appreciate and help those in the military," said David. "Especially in terms of their willingness to sacrifice for something they believed in."

Their work was full of paradoxes. Their convictions about working for pacifism and peace became clearer as they worked with soldiers. David recalled how when asked why they did the work with soldiers in Germany, MJ had once responded, "Because we are Christians." MJ went from helping US soldiers to helping Congolese soldiers lay down their arms, David said.

The accolades and stories continued as the focus shifted to MJ's work with Mennonite Central Committee in the DRC. Tim Lind, who had watched MJ learn to know the Congo while country director with his wife Suzanne, said that while much had been made of MJ's work with armed groups, "it should not be lost that his very foundational experience there was with down-to-earth people displaced by conflict."

"Today there are many women hoeing in their cornfields and many children reciting in primary and secondary schools in Congo who mourn MJ's death," Tim said. He added that MJ was a peacemaker in the tradition of his Anabaptist roots, but also expanded that with his methods.

Suzanne remembered him as smart, witty, and headstrong, but never disrespectful or demeaning. He wasn't always happy, she said. He needed a group of close, fun, nurturing, intelligent friends. "That was hard to find in eastern Congo," she said. He worked at it, but she had worried about him and his well-being as one of his many motherly figures in the world.

Suzanne and Tim had last seen MJ in December as he worked for the United Nations. On March 7, 2017, she had seen that he was on Skype and sent off a greeting. He replied in a vague, kind way, but without the jokes or sparkle she had come to expect from him. "Remember I'm thinking of you a lot and hoping for work and friends you love in your life," she had said.

He replied, "Thank you. All good thoughts are appreciated."

MJ was awed by beauty and moved by the horror in the world. "He gave it his heart, even though he often felt alone and unfinished. As do we all today," Suzanne said before sitting down.

Moussa Ba praised MJ's work with the UN and what he meant to coworkers. "The UN has lost one of its brightest talents," he said, touting MJ's investigatory skills, his passion for peace in Congo, and even his ability to hot-wire a car. "John and Michele, you raised an amazing young man. We are indebted to you for sharing him with us," he said.

The four remaining members of the UN Group of Experts rose and gathered around John and Michele at the front as Zobel Behalal, acting coordinator of the group, presented the parents with two framed photos—one of the last meeting of the experts in New York and the other of the Security Council standing to honor MJ and Zaida.

John and Michele hugged each one of the four experts.

₪ ₪ ₪ ₪

Rachel Sweet, a researcher who worked with MJ in the Congo and also traveled with him in the summer of 2016 to the Boundary Waters and then to Albuquerque, reflected on his complexities and paradoxes. He had a keen mind, and also compassion. He was a Mennonite who loved whiskey.

His work impressed others and left a mark. She quoted a number of unnamed friends and colleagues who touted his work, how he raised rabbits, how he was known as the "mzungu motard" (the white guy with the motorcycle).

She quoted him as saying, "Peace is not kumbaya . . . It's rewarding when something kind of works the way you hope. It's not something that happens a lot. There are many steps backward."

"To choose Congo is to choose heartbreak," said Rachel, quoting a dear friend of MJ's in the Congo. "To love the Congo is to commit to heartbreak. I chose it. I still choose it. As MJ chose it. As Zaida chose it. Because it is love. And only love can do this," the friend had written.

As she began the main meditation, Doreen Miller, MJ's aunt and a spiritual director, asked a simple question. "Where was God?" She urged people to ask God rather than try to figure it out alone, and she shared that she and MJ had questioned God together.

A spiritual connection had formed between the two in autumn 2015, she said. She emailed him regularly and talked with him at length at family gatherings. "We were both suffering deeply as a result of living out our callings from God," she said.

He was suffering because of the evil, violence, and injustice he saw. "It's hard to see God in a field of machete massacre victims or in the person who perpetrated those massacres," he wrote to her in an email in October 2015.

In answering her questions about where God was, she said God was in the love—the 1 Corinthians 13 kind, not the mushy, fuzzy, yellow-smiley-face kind of love. She said God was also in MJ's calling to Anabaptist peacemaking. "Costly discipleship, nonresistance to violence, the expectation of suffering and martyrdom, and forgiveness of enemies have always been central to the way we as Mennonites think and the way we choose to act," she said.

Finding forgiveness for those who killed her nephew, who persecuted him, isn't easy, she said. Yet he had been living out Jesus' Sermon on the Mount, Doreen said. He was working at what Anabaptists call the "upside-down kingdom."

After more than two and a half hours, MJ's service ended with a benediction and the powerful singing of the extended version of the doxology "Praise God from Whom All Blessings Flow," sometimes affectionately called "the Mennonite national anthem" in the United States, sung a cappella in four-part harmony.

Christoph Vogel, who had heard of Mennonites from MJ but never experienced them in this way, said he was impressed by the decency and honor of the service. "It was a very strong moment because I saw this kind of community solidarity within the Mennonite community, which I've heard of from MJ, of course. I got to also see that," he said. He and others were welcomed by the community, including to the meal after the service.

After that meal, the stories continued. There was that summer when MJ was twelve and was the beloved boy at camp and had girls swooning. That time he broke a lock trying to pick it in Albuquerque. That classic story of how he hacked the bell system at Bethany Christian.

And when it was done, people changed into more comfortable clothes and started gathering elsewhere.

A few folks ended up in the basement at Tim Huber's house. The two had been coworkers in Germany and Tim now lived in Newton. Those gathered drank the home-brewed red ale he had on tap and made conversation around the firepit in his backyard and in the basement amid the Hubers' collections of Smurfs and Transformers.

Hesston has few spots for a late-night crowd to gather, even on a Saturday, so many of MJ's friends found their way to nearby Newton. "We just flooded Applebee's," said Andy. "They were completely unprepared for it." At least one person ordered a White Russian, the drink preferred by the Dude in *The Big Lebowski*, to honor MJ.

Andy was exhausted. He hadn't been able to eat during the day, and conversations at the restaurant kept him from ordering. After a couple left the restaurant with half a sandwich still on their plate, he grabbed it and ate it before the server could clear the table.

These friends, dazed by the events of the past weeks, were saying goodbye to MJ together over beers and cheeseburgers. Even after they left Applebee's some of them went to the hotel lobby and talked some more. "We just kind of sat around like sad people, just trying to catch up. Like, 'Did this happen or what?'" Andy said.

₪ ₪ ₪ ₪

The next morning, about fifty people gathered for brunch at John and Michele's house. For hours, those who knew MJ told stories that evoked belly laughs. As the stories flowed, so did tears. MJ was a storyteller, a gift he inherited from his father, and now others told these stories, enough to fill a life and more than enough to fill a book.

MJ's former longtime girlfriend Hannah van Bebber sat next to Timo Mueller, with whom MJ had walked over roughly 125 miles in the Congo to have an adventure and embrace the country in which they were living and working. Timo told of that walk along Lake Kivu over eight days. They became minor celebrities, awaited by villagers, as they walked. One of the Congolese mothers offered to carry them because they looked tired, Timo said. At night, they would meet with local leaders, trying to explain why they were walking. MJ exercised what he called his "Mennonite diplomacy," Timo said.

Patrick Maxwell told of MJ, wearing nothing but boxer shorts and flip-flops, trying to kill a rooster in their home in Bukavu, Congo.

Andy could picture his friend chasing the rooster that night, could picture him with these people in the Congo. These stories that were new but involved this familiar person were special to him. "You're able to find your friend in this other place," Andy said.

As Sunday morning turned into early afternoon, the stories continued to flow as people left the Sharps' to catch flights or start driving. They were returning to their routines and their lives—without this man they loved and from whom they had learned so much.

After Keith and Andy took Rachel Sweet to the airport, the two sat in a Subway down the road from the Sharp house. Nick Gingerich, Andy's cousin and part of the group of high school friends, joined them. "We just sat there and started joking around," Andy said. It felt like old times, as if they'd gone back to a simpler time, before the pain of MJ's death. It was great to sit as if he were there with them, eating a sandwich.

They got in the van to head back to the Sharps' house and passed a gas station.

"No way, dude," Keith said to Andy, who was in the passenger's seat of the van.

At the gas pump was a creamy white Porsche 944 from the early 1980s. It was nearly identical to the one MJ used to drive.

Keith had been looking for a Porsche like MJ's, and here was such a car. "I don't know about signs from beyond. I'm not a person given to taking that too far," Andy said. "But, man, what are the chances this guy is filling up with gas at this gas station between where we are coming and where we are going in the middle of Kansas? We were driving a quarter mile back to the Sharps. We just couldn't believe this car showed up."

The owner came out of the gas station carrying Mountain Dew and food, and saw the two of them losing their minds over his car.

"Dude, you've gotta sell me this car," Keith said.

"No, I love this car," the man said.

MJ likely could have convinced him, but Keith couldn't. The man drove off in that white Porsche.

By this time, Keith was laughing. Andy was crying.

Keith said it was a God moment "or whatever," a moment when he felt that things would be okay even without MJ. Andy said he felt close to MJ right then.

Not much was open Easter Sunday, but Andy and Keith found a bowling alley in Wichita. Others joined them as they spent the evening the way they would have with MJ.

Keith usually won when they went bowling. On this day, Andy won. "I told Keith I thought MJ let me do it," Andy said, "just to piss him off."

Lose your life and you will save it. Submit to death, death of our ambitions and favorite wishes every day, and death to your whole body in the end: submit with every fiber of your being, and you will find eternal life. Keep back nothing. Nothing that you have not given away will be really yours. Nothing in you that has not died will be raised from the dead. Look for yourself, and you will find in the long run only hatred, loneliness, despair, rage, ruin, and decay. But look for Christ and you will find him, and with him everything else thrown in.

—**C. S. LEWIS**, Mere Christianity

THIRTEEN

Seeking Justice

THE EARLY NEWS ACCOUNTS of MJ's and Zaida's deaths included a number of inaccuracies. Some said that the body of their local interpreter Betu Tshinsela was also discovered. Others said that he and the three motorcycle drivers were killed. The truth is their fates remain unknown and they may have been part of the plot or joined it unknowingly.

FARDC officers were the source of some of the confusion. One claimed that MJ and Zaida had been kidnapped and were alive before changing his story several days later.

What is known is that MJ and Zaida passed through at least two FARDC checkpoints on the day of their death and then one militia checkpoint before being stopped at another. They were abducted, stripped of their shoes and most of their belongings, and led to the place of their executions. Those FARDC officers implicated local chiefs. The mystery of what happened swirled into an opaque dust storm.

Swedish authorities launched an investigation into Zaida's death almost immediately after her body was found. Minister of Education Gustav Fridolin, who had worked with Zaida in the Young Greens of Sweden, commented on her death, as did the prime minister Stefan Löfven.

In the United States, President Donald J. Trump had taken office just months before, and there was no comment from the Oval Office, as there might have been under another administration. There was no call for an investigation or calls for justice emerging from the White House. Trump made clear his disdain for the UN and certain countries around the world. The sitting US president used a vulgarity to refer to African nations and Haiti.

At the UN offices in New York and Washington, D.C., as well as at the State Department, those who worked with MJ were grieving and struggling to separate fact from fiction. Those offices rely on reports from the field, from people on the ground doing an investigation. Someone like MJ had the skills to do an investigation into a death such as his, but as Julie Jolles put it, "The UN's experience and forte is not in solving murders, and the politics inherent in the structure of the UN make it particularly ill-suited for a quick and fully transparent investigation."

The members of the Group of Experts who had just lost colleagues were also reeling. They still had a mandate and somehow managed to complete reports later that year for the UN Security Council.

On April 23, just eight days after MJ's funeral, Joseph Kabila's government in Kinshasa invited reporters to a press conference at which they showed a six-minute, seventeen-second video of MJ's and Zaida's shooting deaths and then men cutting Zaida's head off her body. The UN and the families had not even known the video existed.

The government showed the video to blame the Kamuina Nsapu for the deaths, and news outlets across the world carried its message. In the DRC, video is used as a weapon of war. In the battle between the Congolese government and the Kamuina Nsapu, videos have been used to assign blame for the horrors. Government spokesman Lambert Mende said, "Our police and soldiers are accused of being implicated in the assassination of the two UN experts. That is not the case. The images speak for themselves. It is not our soldiers that we see in the video executing the two UN workers but the terrorists of the Kamuina Nsapu militia."[1]

The press conference also included a video of beheaded bodies wearing police uniforms, attributing that action to the Kamuina Nsapu as well.

The video of MJ's and Zaida's executions quickly spread, including on social media. "Our colleagues in the DRC [Democratic Republic of the Congo] have seen the video and we are utterly horrified at what appears to be the killing of Michael Sharp and Zaida Catalán," said UN human rights spokeswoman Ravina Shamdasani in an article in *The Guardian*.[2]

The video is horrific, and it had tremendous power. It eliminated some of the mysteries of what happened on March 12, though many questions still remain.

ℶ ℶ ℶ ℶ

In the weeks that followed, the families of MJ and Zaida, along with others who had known them, discussed the best approach to advocate for investigations into the deaths and find the truth of what happened.

The first efforts were to ask those in the US Congress to pressure UN ambassador Nikki Haley to ensure that UN secretary-general António Guterres would commission a special investigation. The goal was to identify the real perpetrators and chain of command for the killings.

A group of Mennonite peacemakers and Congolese advocates helped MJ's family and friends start contacting their senators and representatives, as well as foreign relations/affairs committee members in the two US legislative houses. Together the group created a script offering tips on the best way to advocate for accountability. "Let's ensure that Michael and Zaida's deaths are not in vain by continuing to protect the mission they died for: bringing truth of injustice to light," it read. In June 2017, John and Michele wrote a letter to US senator Cory Booker, asking him to help. They also sent a letter to Secretary-General Guterres, who had sent them a letter of condolence. They told him, "We continue to muse about the shape of justice in this case. Can there be redemption in the process, redemption that would improve the lives of millions of Congolese to which Michael dedicated his life? Whatever the outcome, we wish for accountability. Seeking accountability surely begins with a thorough investigation. Please know that we will continue to press for a special commissioned criminal investigation that is independent and international and could work in cooperation with country investigations."

Around the same time that MJ and Zaida died, US and UN officials had been raising alarms about the violence in Kasai. The crimes against women and children were being documented, but how to respond was less clear.

Nikki Haley, the former governor of South Carolina, had become the new US ambassador to the United Nations in January 2017. She was savvy about what she said publicly but was also willing to speak her mind. She and others were privately starting to call for action.

US diplomats were pressuring the UN behind the scenes to investigate the deaths of the experts as well as others in Kasai. Guterres appointed Greg Starr, a US diplomat who had been an assistant secretary of state for diplomatic security and UN under-secretary-general for safety and security, to conduct a Board of Inquiry into the deaths.

Starr started meeting with people at the UN and State Department and had a call with MJ's and Zaida's families around the beginning of June. John and Michele pointed him to MJ's computer, which was in the hands of the FBI along with several handwritten journals. They told him about those who had helped search for MJ. They told him that a linguistic analysis of the death video had already been done and cited how he could find it.

John and Michele were hopeful that the investigation would point toward justice, but not revenge.

As Starr began his investigation, he scrutinized whether MJ and Zaida followed protocols and the security measures that the UN had in place—always a point of tension between people in the field and those inside the institution.

Starr and his team spent two weeks in Kinshasa and Kananga. They communicated with people at the UN and at the State Department as they conducted their investigation.

When Starr spoke to family members in July, the Sharp and Moresby families not only took notes, but also recorded the conversation, already unsure whether they could trust Starr because of what he was saying about his investigation. On the call, he offered his theories of what happened, including his doubts that FARDC was responsible or that the government forces assisted others in carrying out the deaths. He told them that it was likely that Kamuina Nsapu had killed the duo and that the people in the video would be identified. He said that MJ and Zaida were within their charter to investigate, but may not have known how dangerous it was. He said that the linguistic analysis of the video was inconclusive and that he had turned everything over to the FBI.

₪ ₪ ₪ ₪

Starr's report was classified, but bits of it leaked to the press after it was issued on August 15, 2017.

Nikki Haley issued a statement saying that the Board of Inquiry report was the first step in the pursuit of justice for the murders of MJ and Zaida and that a full investigation of the deaths and who was accountable was still needed. "There is simply no other appropriate course of action," it stated.[3]

Others were more pointed in their critique. Christoph Vogel, Sonia Rolley, and others were quick to criticize Starr's work. He didn't interview a number of people who had already done work to find out what happened, including Rolley and Emmanuel Billay.

John Sharp said that Starr had said that "they operated like cowboys." Starr denied saying that, but others heard him make colorful assessments of the situation as he did the work. Four times in the report, Starr criticized MJ and Zaida's use of motorcycles, noting that using non-UN vehicles without an escort allowed "bad actors" to carry out their deaths.

Starr also dismissed the possible role of the Congolese government in the deaths. "It is the judgment of the Board that information circulating regarding the possible involvement of various government individuals or organizations, does not provide proof of intent or motive on the part of any individual(s)," said the report.

Both families were alarmed by what Starr produced, and they felt betrayed. "Blaming the victim is the oldest cop-out in the world," John told interviewers in an award-winning documentary *Deceptive Diplomacy*[4] produced by Mission Investigate, a consortium of journalists from *Foreign Policy*, Radio France Internationale, *Le Monde*, Sveriges Television, and *Süddeutsche Zeitung* who collaborated on stories as well as the documentary.

In the months after Starr's report was released, all the documents he used were leaked from the UN to reporters. The

Mission Investigate journalists, using their own research and the leaked materials from Starr's investigation, were able to put together a more nuanced, and likely far more accurate, picture of what happened on March 11 and 12.

They obtained the UN documents from people inside the organization who were appalled by the situation, said Rolley, whose journalism for Radio France Internationale has gotten her banned from the DRC since April 2017.

The documents showed that the Congolese military had infiltrated the Kamuina Nsapu and that intelligence agents, including those acting as translators on March 11, had played a role in MJ's and Zaida's deaths in order to prevent them from revealing the military's mass graves. The UN's translation of Zaida's secret recording of the meeting at Wood Land Guest House showed that the translators had lied to lead the UN workers into a trap.

While Starr left this information out of his report, Rolley and others stepped forward to reveal the truth. MJ's and Zaida's families criticized Starr for leaving out the information and lying to them. The families said that Starr told them he didn't want the report to keep the Congolese government from working with others on investigations. He didn't mention the lie MJ and Zaida were told at the hotel about their safety the next day, though he had a transcription of the meeting. He didn't include the forty-five calls between Col. Jean de Dieu Mambweni and Congolese armed forces that day, including one at 5:25 p.m. that used the same tower that routed the 4:49 p.m. call from Zaida's phone. Nor did he mention that MJ's phone was used months after his death.

Rolley, who is highly critical of the UN in general, said the Starr report was a negotiation instrument to get the Congolese government to cooperate. She wants to find the truth, to hold people accountable. Her reporting, including details that cast significant doubt on whether those in the execution video are actually all members of Kamuina Nsapu, as previously thought, continues to shed light on what really happened on March 12.

After Mission Investigate showed that Col. Mambweni lied under oath about his phone usage on the day of the murders, he was arrested in December 2018 and months later was charged with MJ's and Zaida's murders, according to numerous press reports.

In May 2020, Rolley reported that a former Kamuina Nsapu militia chief who was wanted for his involvement in the deaths was arrested in Kananga. Even if the steps are small, she persists in continuing the work.

The court system in the DRC functions slowly, if at all. A witness to the murders of MJ and Zaida was poisoned in his cell in October 2018. Trials are rare, and justice even rarer. Yet the families continue to call for steps toward justice on the international level.

MJ's mother Michele said in the documentary, "I don't think you have to lie to be diplomatic." As she and John were processing what Starr's report said, they were already doing their own form of diplomacy.

₪ ₪ ₪ ₪

On August 17, 2017, the same day that Haley issued the statement on the Starr report, John and Michele were sitting in her UN office in New York.

They had traveled to the New York headquarters at the invitation of the UN Security Council. Elizabeth and Maria Moresby had also traveled to New York as guests of the council.

They sat in the front row of the council meeting as fourteen of the fifteen permanent and temporary member nations gave formal tributes to the two who had been killed.

The Russian representative had expressed condolences to the Sharps beforehand, but in the meeting complimented Kabila's government for its cooperation with investigations, including the FBI.

After the meeting, Michele walked up to the man, who was joined by the Russian ambassador, and told him, "Everything you said, it was not true."

She had simply confronted him, but graciously. He apologized to her. "Oh, we're so sorry, we didn't know," he said.

Arrangements were made for John and Michele to meet with the foreign minister from the Democratic Republic of the Congo if they wished. US diplomats protested, but John said, "What can it hurt?"

Julie Jolles was anxious about what would transpire and posted staff nearby to intervene if needed. Then she heard laughter coming from behind the closed door where they were meeting. After the meeting ended, those in the room took photos together. Julie remembers, "Mrs. Sharp looks over to John and says, 'I think we accomplished what we wanted to accomplish.'"

Like their son, they were building peace. That's hard work. "It's really easy to think, 'Oh, I want to create world peace and go hold hands with Israelis and Palestinians,'" Julie said. Peacebuilding starts by listening to someone—an armed soldier or a foreign diplomat—and becomes loving your neighbor.

Julie said, "There are a lot of humanitarians and peacemakers who do not live up to their principles. They get a lot of press, but they don't practice what they preach. Michael and the Sharps are some of the people that fully embody the beliefs they espouse."

Julie said she learned so much from watching the Sharps, and that MJ would be so proud of them and their approach to peacemaking, even around his death.

Secretary-General António Guterres assured John and Michele and the Moresbys when they met with him that the UN would pursue an investigation—for MJ and Zaida and for those who would work for the UN in the future. On another visit, MJ's sisters Laura and Erin attended the annual memorial service held at UN Headquarters to honor all UN personnel who lost their lives in the service of peace during the previous year. They met with Secretary Guterres, Ambassador Haley, and other officials and heard from colleagues about the impact MJ had on their lives and work.

John and Michele have continued to call for justice in the form of arrests, a trial, and some sort of accountability. They don't want revenge. They don't want the perpetrators to die for what they did any more than MJ wanted that for the armed militia leaders he was pressured to hand over.

They just want the killers to be named and held to account for what they did, the same way that MJ worked for that on behalf of the UN as the armed groups expert and coordinator of the Group of Experts over two mandates.

In the fall of 2017, Haley traveled to Africa and visited the DRC with several other international officials. She describes the visit in her book *With All Due Respect: Defending America with Grit and Grace*. She writes about how President Kabila was stalling on elections and how crimes continued to be committed against the Congolese people. "Even UN officials investigating human rights abuses were being killed," she writes.[5]

One of the reasons Haley went to the DRC was because MJ had died. "Nikki didn't get mad about voting machines," said Julie Jolles referencing the Congolese election. "She got mad about Michael Sharp."

At that meeting, Haley gave Kabila a list of the men who were known to be involved, based on the evidence in the video of the executions. In February 2018, Haley created headlines at the UN when she asked the Congolese foreign minister Léonard She Okitundu during a UN meeting what Kabila had done with the list of names she had provided.

"Please ask Mr. Kabila what he did with my list," she said. "I gave [the president] a list, and no action has been taken. That list is what we know needs to be looked at, and it is a serious list in reference to the deaths of those two people."[6]

The US Mission to the UN contended that Kabila and the DRC government hadn't done anything to seriously investigate and arrest those involved. Okitundu said that they were investigating and there must be a fair trial, yet there was little evidence that Kabila and his people were doing anything other than placating those calling for a trial.

₪ ₪ ₪ ₪

The deaths of MJ and Zaida have remained an international murder mystery for more than five years.

Who really killed them, and why?

Robert Petit, whom the UN appointed in October 2017 to lead a team of international investigators, has gotten closer to answers than Starr did, but has been hampered by DRC officials. Petit led an investigation into senior leaders of the Khmer Rouge in Cambodia thirty years after their war crimes. He is in regular contact with the Sharp and Moresby families.

When MJ and Zaida went missing, Ida Sawyer at Human Rights Watch listened to people calling it a government plot. She, too, had a gut feeling that the DRC intelligence services and military were somehow responsible.

The government's explanation of the video didn't make sense to her, and she has sources who say that the senior levels of the intelligence service worked with local residents in the Kasais to kill the two.

It altered how she thinks about working in the DRC. "This really changes my calculation and I imagine the calculation of many other people operating in the Congo," she said. "And also what's so maddening is that at least until now they've gotten away with it and we haven't yet seen justice and those most responsible held to account."

Emmanuel Billay, who worked alongside MJ for five years, said that Kabila transferred conflict to Kasai to extend his grip on power. The chaos benefited him when he claimed that he couldn't conduct an election.

Ida Sawyer, who worked in the DRC from January 2008 until August 2016, when DRC officials banned her from the country for her criticism, said, "They seemed more and more willing to do what it takes to maintain their grip on power."

Violence between the government forces and the Kamuina Nsapu intensified and resulted in thousands of deaths. Another 1.4 million people, including 850,000 children, were forced from their homes in the five provinces in the center of the country. Congolese Mennonites in the region were killed or displaced. Some individuals experienced gruesome violence. Many of the 235,000 Mennonites in the Congo did all they could to offer aid and help those who were displaced.

The government insisted that the militia group was responsible even as evidence grew that it may have been orchestrating much of the violence itself. Ida Sawyer came to believe that for the government, "there was a fear that Michael and Zaida would uncover this and change the narrative."

Jason Stearns said MJ was doing his job—and not recklessly. This wasn't a situation that spiraled out of control. Jason said he can't imagine that the Kamuina Nsapu wanted to kill white people for no reason, as the government has alleged. "The likeliest explanation in my mind is that it was the Congolese government that did it," he said.

Did it go all the way to Kabila? We may never know. As president, Kabila would play people or groups against each other and use co-option to hold on to his power. He would repress those who protested sometimes to the point of death, but assassinations weren't a significant tool in his toolbox, said Jason.

What happened in the Kasais, an area with grinding poverty, was a rare and unique situation, even in the DRC. But somehow, someone planned the deaths of these two peacemakers and has yet to be held accountable.

₪ ₪ ₪ ₪

Zaida's ashes are buried in a cemetery next to a premedieval era church just down the road from her mother's house on the island of Öland. Maria and her daughter Elizabeth visit often. On a June day in 2018, I visited with them, watching as they lovingly cleaned the granite marker and tidied around it. The headstone has an angel and the words "Per aspera ad astra," just like the tattoo on Zaida's wrist. The breeze from the sea off the southeast coast of Sweden often washes over the cemetery.

MJ's ashes have traveled the world, almost needing their own passport. People in the inner circle of friends and family each got some ashes to spread. "I've lost count how many places I've spread ashes," Andy said.

Family and friends spread ashes on a hilltop in Harrisonburg, Virginia, above the campus where MJ went to college. When they looked at the photos they took that day, there were unexplained points of light on the ground where the ashes lay.

Some were spread in Hesston, on a mountain near Albuquerque, and at the Sharp family farm in Belleville, Pennsylvania.

On the first day of a canoe trip of family and close friends in the summer of 2018, eight of us followed the same course

John Sharp spreads his son MJ's ashes on the top of Mount Kilimanjaro in 2019. PHOTO BY CHRISTY KAUFFMAN, USED BY PERMISSION

MJ had taken with Andy and Keith as teenagers. Four canoes paused just past a portage trail. Andy pulled out a bag of MJ's ashes and each person put a bit in their hand before releasing the ashes into the brown water at the spot where the friends had caught more than a hundred fish on the trip seventeen years earlier. That trip at the end of high school marked the end of their being kids together, said Andy.

"I think this is a place where MJ would be okay to be," said Keith to the rest of the group. "I'm so thankful to share this place with you guys."

Erin sniffled and cried. John wept into his hat, one that MJ had brought back from Costa Rica, after he released the ashes of his son. Tears ran down my face as I held MJ's ashes and released them into the water.

A few nights later, the group spread more ashes along the shore of the campsite. There were more tears, and since this time the group wasn't separated by canoes, those who had loved MJ could share hugs and hold each other in the silence along- side a beautiful lake as the sun set.

The next morning, as the group departed, a fishing pole, probably still strung with a torpedo lure, remained behind at that campsite. We had miscommunicated about who was responsible to put it in the canoe. We discussed going back but opted to leave it.

"It feels right to leave a pole with MJ," Keith said.

I told him, "I hope a ten-year-old kid finds it, grinning from ear to ear, wondering at the possibility."

An unrealized dream of MJ's ended up inspiring a trek to scatter his ashes. MJ had talked with friends about wanting to hike Kilimanjaro. Wilmer Otto, a friend of John's, helped organize "MJ's Dream Hike" up the mountain to summit around the two-year anniversary of the deaths in March 2019.

The climb to the "roof of Africa" became a fundraiser for the Michael J. Sharp Peace and Justice Endowed Scholarship at the Center for Justice and Peacebuilding at MJ's college alma mater, EMU.

John and eleven others, including EMU students working on a documentary about MJ and people who worked with MJ in the DRC, climbed the mountain and raised $137,979 for the scholarship. The university worked with the family and close friends to establish the scholarship at the school's peacebuilding institute. As of 2021, it helps a Congolese student attend the institute, and those close to MJ help manage the scholarship in his honor.

After summiting the peak, John let his son's ashes float from his fingers at the top of the mountain.

₪ ₪ ₪ ₪

MJ and Zaida live on in artwork, in tributes, in the way people continue to remember and honor them.

In the months after their deaths, Lisa Mast, who attended EMU with MJ and was at the time coordinating the University of New Mexico Men's Choir in Albuquerque, had the choir sing three pieces in tribute to him. "I couldn't do anything to save MJ. None of us could. But I had to do something," said Lisa.

Many people who knew MJ and Zaida have created tributes using a variety of mediums. In 2021, artist Paul Friesen created a sculpture in honor of MJ using a piece of king ebony wood he had been given in the mid-1960s that was awaiting the right inspiration. As he worked, the ninety-seven-year-old meditated on 2 Corinthians 4:7–12, which inspired the words "though we be persecuted, we are not forgotten."

Thommy Bremberg, a Swedish artist working in Italy, made a sculpture of a large bullet with a drop of blood entitled *Abused Ammunition* that became part of the UN's permanent art collection. "MJ's and Zaida's dreams for a peaceful world are stronger and brighter than the bullets that killed them," said John Sharp.

In addition to the EMU scholarship honoring MJ, two scholarships honor Zaida, including one awarded by the Network on Humanitarian Action. In February 2018 the Chilean Embassy in Sweden named a room for her.

Both MJ and Zaida were given the Dag Hammarskjöld Medal. UN Secretary-General Hammarskjöld died in September 1961 when his plane crashed mysteriously as he was visiting the Congo to negotiate a ceasefire. The medal is given to those who have lost their lives as a result of UN peacekeeping work.

In the DRC, Moise Butimbushi, MJ's friend and coworker, has continued to gather people to remember MJ. He led a ceremony marking the fourth anniversary of the deaths. He also named a newborn son Michael, as did another family who knew MJ.

In American Mennonite circles, MJ was the first to be given the EMU Life Service Award in the fall of 2017. His parents accepted the award in his place. They often spoke together publicly about their son, particularly in the first year.

In the summer of 2019, they spoke via video to the youth convention of the Mennonite Church USA gathering, urging the young people to take risks and be peacemakers. John spoke to several gatherings of youth and adults at the 2021 Mennonite Church USA convention in Cincinnati and told them to do things that are significant enough that they would be willing to risk their lives for them.

John has continued to speak often to churches or other groups about his son who "lived as he died: fully engaged."

But the tribute that might please MJ the most is one at Goshen Brewing, the home of Menno-Mighty, where a beer named School Bell Stout was created in MJ's honor—a playful nod to his prank of ringing the high school bells. Keith Grubaugh helped come up with the idea for honoring MJ in that way, and MJ's friend Justin Ramer and his sister Erin's friend Jesse Sensenig are two of the owner/operators at the brewery who made it happen.

The first pints sold in August 2019 raised $15,000 for MJ's scholarship fund. Any time the beer brewed with Congolese coffee is on tap, a portion of the sales are sent to EMU for the fund.

Those who were close to MJ appreciate the tributes and honors, yet they'd trade them all to have MJ alive.

Andy and Keith have said that they still have survivor's guilt.

"I would have paid [the shooter] so much money not to pull that trigger," said Keith.

"All that I have," added his father John.

Love in action is a harsh and dreadful thing compared with love in dreams. Love in dreams is greedy for immediate action, rapidly performed and in the sight of all. Men will even give their lives if only the ordeal does not last long but is soon over, with all looking on and applauding as though on the stage. But active love is labor and fortitude.

—FYODOR DOSTOYEVSKY, _The Brothers Karamazov_

FOURTEEN

What's a Hero?

IT'S RARE TO be willing to sacrifice yourself for a stranger.

Brian Palmer is a social anthropologist and scholar of religion at Uppsala University in Sweden and has studied dozens of people who have demonstrated this quality. He taught about it in his classes at Harvard University, where he got his doctoral degree, and now in Sweden, where he encountered a young Zaida. "I sense that Zaida was a person of considerable compassion for others, of great empathy already from childhood," he said.

Brian has cowritten a book of 101 stories of people who have sacrificed for others, many of them losing their own lives.[1] The book tells the stories of Rosa Parks, Mahatma Gandhi, and Martin Luther King Jr., as well as the tale of Maximilian Kolbe, who offered to take the place of a husband and father at Auschwitz. The man he saved lived until the 1990s.

Before her death, Zaida would speak to Brian's students as a living example of the civic courage in which he so strongly

believes. Her honesty and directness about injustice was strik-
ing, and his students were moved when she visited.

"Courage can almost be as contagious as fear when one
meets someone face-to-face who is taking risks," he said.

The people who show courage on behalf of others give Brian
hope for the world, helping him believe the world is not as
brutal as it often seems.

"I see these lives as both beautiful and tragic when someone
is ready to risk their lives for strangers. In some ways, nothing
that humans do is more beautiful," he said.

MJ and Zaida knew the risks yet acted generously. Brian has
sometimes wished that Zaida had been less courageous. That's
often a dilemma for those who take risks—those who love them
want them to be safe, and sometimes that is in tension with the
actions their courage inspires.

"They knew there were risks in doing that work for anybody and were ready to take those risks," said Brian. "That
story can remind us that it is possible for human beings to
be so beautiful that our lives can have much richer and more
generous purposes than simply advancing our own careers
or accumulating a lot of wealth and comfort. So much of
what's human and decent and caring in the world is owing
to people who generation after generation have been willing
to care about others so deeply that they paid a price in their
own lives."

ℵ ℵ ℵ ℵ

Many have questioned whether MJ and Zaida should have
traveled to and in Kasai-Central to investigate.

Greg Starr questioned whether MJ and Zaida knew what
they were doing, whether they were following protocols. Others
have noted they were unarmed and had no one with them to
protect them.

Questioning their decision after their deaths is too easy for those living a comfortable life with little risk.

It is true that they might still be alive if they hadn't gone. But that wasn't the life they were choosing.

The better question is, How could they not go?

At the time, there was growing international pressure to find out what was truly happening in this remote part of the world. Children were being killed as victims of war. A nation's armed forces were killing women and children and recording it on video.

And then there were MJ and Zaida themselves. They were both passionate about their work, starting in their years of peacebuilding in the United States and Sweden, in the Middle East, Afghanistan, Germany, and ultimately in the Democratic Republic of the Congo.

Passion doesn't automatically translate to wisdom and good judgment, but they were taking precautions. To not go to Kasai-Central would have been going against their preparation, their training, and their concern for the people they were trying to help.

MJ assessed risk his entire life.

When he enacted the bell prank at Bethany, he was calculating the risk of getting caught.

When he played poker at casinos and with the soldiers and officers at German military bases, he was measuring the risk and often winning.

When he was helping Agustín Aguayo and Robert Weiss live out their convictions, he was taking into account the risk for them and for himself if they went AWOL.

When he went to meet with the leaders of armed groups, men who may have been involved in genocide, he took into account not just his safety but that of those who walked alongside to help him get there.

Annie Duke, a former professional poker player who made more than $4 million in tournaments, wrote a book about making better choices in which she says that luck and the quality of your decisions determine how your life turns out.[2] "We tend to think of decisions as being right or wrong as opposed to in-between," she said in a magazine story. "The way we figure out if it is right or wrong is if it worked out or not. The problem is that just because something worked out well or poorly, it doesn't tell you if the decision was good or not."[3]

MJ, with others, was trying to protect the children of the Congo, the men and women caught in violence. He was doing that work when he died. That work arose out of his commitment to nonviolence, out of his belief in a loving God and his own sense that he could make a difference.

MJ visits with Elizabeth Namavu and children in Mubimbi Camp, home to displaced persons in the Democratic Republic of the Congo. PHOTO BY JANA AŠENBRENNEROVÁ, USED BY PERMISSION OF MENNONITE CENTRAL COMMITTEE

Ben Weisbrod, the MCC area director who invited MJ to join him on vacation over Christmas 2014, said that MJ was a humble human imitating Christ. Ben told me in an email after our interview, "The Mennonite experience includes so many things but at a deep level it includes a scripture passage like Philippians 2:7 and imagining Jesus and you and what it means to take on life, become a life, put on flesh or garments within a context of real life. Imitation of Christ—in humility. So here I am doing the thing I resist, summing up that which is hard to sum up. But I think you know the point I'm wishing to make: Michael, taking on risk? Let's get this straight. Michael took on life, wrapped himself in life being lived."

₪ ₪ ₪ ₪

Julie Jolles left the large meeting room at the UN offices in New York just after the Security Council passed the new MONUSCO resolution to keep soldiers in the DRC.

The negotiations leading up to the vote were underway in March 2017. They were tense. The deaths of MJ and Zaida had delayed the vote.

As Julie walked out of the room, she saw a bird, perhaps a pigeon, sitting on one of the chairs outside the room.

She believes that if you find a bird in your house after someone dies and the bird is alive, the person's spirit is free. Julie looked at the bird and said, "Michael, you've gotta give me a break."

She remembers that bird, that moment, as somehow representing MJ's presence.

In his life, MJ couldn't bring about all the change he wanted. Nor can he in his death, though he was right that his death and that of Zaida would bring attention to the plight of people in the DRC.

Julie thinks of how he longed for justice in the DRC and that an election that actually happened in late 2018, people being arrested for Zaida's and his deaths, and a trial that isn't a complete sham *is* progress. She had very low expectations that anyone would ever be held accountable or that we would ever know what happened.

"I told the Sharps this when we first met. I was, happily, proven wrong," she said. "I recognize that the investigations and trial do not meet any international standards, but on day one we thought we would never find the bodies. The discovery of the bodies, the video, the creation of the follow-on mechanism, the phone logs, the change of the DRC government, and the sustained international support for the investigation are successes. Funny, all of those things are data points Michael would have loved to have used in an investigation."

A diplomatic effort the year before MJ's death to have the UN Human Rights Council investigate violence in the Kasais didn't yield anything. MJ and Zaida's investigation did, though it came with great loss.

MJ traveled the world during his life, to the point of needing additional pages in his passport. In the years since his death, MJ's spirit has kept finding his way into "thin space."

Celtic Christians have historically viewed places or moments where space between the physical world and spiritual one is thin enough for people who are living to encounter those who have died.

MJ has done that, sometimes in ways that defy even the boldest imagination. He has appeared in dreams of those who knew him, sometimes so vividly that the dreamers wake up crying, believing they have just encountered him again.

₪ ₪ ₪ ₪

In late 2017, Timo Mueller was at Plum Village, a Buddhist monastery in France, for three months. He needed a place to process after his friend's death and the completion of his own work in the Congo.

Timo was MJ's friend from the DRC, who like him worked to make a difference in that country. The monastics were helping Timo with compassion, to overcome the anger that would separate him from the healing for which he longed.

They suggested that he get up in the morning and go to the dining hall to set a table for himself, for MJ and Zaida, and for the men he saw in the video of their deaths. Timo said he needed to have a relationship, somehow, with the men in the video.

So he set a table for himself and all of them. As he put down every plate, cup, and utensil at nineteen place settings, he said over and over again, "Love and compassion."

He didn't want to befriend the men who had pulled the trigger, who had ended the lives of MJ and Zaida. Yet he also didn't want to be weighed down by the anger he felt.

The practice helped him see that it wasn't just victim and perpetrator. All of those involved were victims somehow in a cycle of violence.

The practice, which Timo did a number of times over several weeks, allowed him to again touch the emotion that had led him to the Congo to do the humanitarian work that he, MJ, and Zaida did.

It was a way of viewing the killers charitably.

With love and compassion.

֍ ֍ ֍ ֍

If you ask John Sharp whether his son was a martyr, he answers, "It's not for me to say."

As a historian, John has a keener understanding than most of what a martyr is, or at least was during the early stages of Anabaptism. He has taught about the martyrs and written about their lives and deaths.

The term *martyr* gets used flippantly in modern American culture, often belying its true meaning.

A martyr is classically defined as someone who chooses to die rather than renounce religious principles. A broader definition could be someone who dies for their beliefs.

Sarah Nahar, who helped link MJ to the MCC job in the Congo, compared MJ to Michael Sattler, the early Anabaptist martyr. "They both nonviolently, strategically, and passionately pushed the boundaries of what most people think is possible for a just society with accountability," she said.

Kambale Musavuli, an advocate and activist on behalf of his home country for Friends of the Congo, said the problem with labeling someone a martyr is that it tends to praise individuals and not the cause of which they were working to remind others. Kambale said, "As they are called martyr, it completely erases the story of the Congolese people."

MJ and Zaida were working to improve lives in the DRC. "They are the symbol of millions who have died because they are a shining light on the issue," he said.

He doubts they would have been okay with being called martyrs. "They were assassinated," he said.

The more interesting question is whether MJ was a hero. Some don't like the word, because it, too, is overused. MJ's friend and professor of international studies Jonathan Moyer asks whether there can even be Mennonite heroes, or if it is an oxymoron. Mennonites don't celebrate pride as a virtue.

Despite MJ's own joking with Hannah van Bebber in Germany, he didn't present himself as a hero. He worked to keep his ego in check. He didn't often tout his own accomplishments around others.

"A hero does heroic stuff because it's the right thing to do, not because it's heroic," said his former Bible teacher Dale Shenk.

MJ certainly wasn't a saint, and would have bristled at the comparison. Superheroes sell better than saints these days anyway. Superheroes are a thriving industry as books and movies celebrate individuals with special talents. The formula is simple: Heroes help others. Villains do damage.

But the narratives of superheroes, even the most popular ones, are misleading, says Brian Palmer, the Swedish researcher on civic courage. "They underestimate the side of loss and grief and mourning and finitude. They make it seem easier and more glamorous than it is," he said.

MJ didn't wear a cape or spin webs. He didn't become a millionaire as some thought he would. He didn't bring lasting peace to the DRC. Yet he used his amazing intellect, quick wit, and passion to make the world better. He saved lives with his words and actions because he was willing to listen first.

When John and Michele met the new DRC president, Félix Tshisekedi, in April 2019, he told them, "Michael and Zaida are heroes in our country. Everybody knows the story and we will never forget them."

Mulanda "Jimmy" Juma took it further than the president of his country. "Michael was a hero in my view in the sense that he was doing the right thing to bring about peace in the Congo, struggling for the protection of human rights, and he was killed for doing the right thing," he told me. "He was killed for protection of human rights and not just for one person. For thousands of people who are unaccounted for."

Being a hero involves sacrifice. MJ told others he did things well because he demanded excellence of himself and was disappointed when he didn't achieve it. That meant that he was sometimes lonely, sometimes depressed, and always human. He was not perfect. He fought long odds and made a difference because of his skill and courage.

If asked whether he was a hero, MJ likely would have answered the same way his father has about martyrdom. "It's not for me to say," he might have said. Or perhaps he would have invoked *The Big Lebowski*. "I won't say a hero, 'cause, what's a hero?"

That doesn't mean he wasn't a hero. And we can debate whether to call him one.

The more important question is whether we will be bold enough to live fully engaged and courageously. As MJ did.

MJ takes in the beauty of the Democratic Republic of the Congo on a hike along Lake Kivu in 2014. PHOTO COURTESY TIMO MUELLER

Glossary of Key People, Places, and Groups

Bammental—A small, historic municipality in the state of Baden-Württemberg in southwest Germany, near the German city of Heidelberg and the border with France.

Bukavu—A city in eastern Democratic Republic of the Congo along the shore of Lake Kivu and near the border with Rwanda. It has a population of around a million people.

Deutsche Mennonitisches Friedenskomitee—The German Mennonite Peace Committee, also known by its acronym DMFK, established in the 1950s by German Mennonites. Its offices are in Bammental.

DRC—The Democratic Republic of the the Congo, formerly known as Zaire, is a country in central Africa. Though the DRC is often called "the Congo," the smaller Republic of the Congo is also in Africa. DRC, also referred to as DR Congo, is one of the world's largest countries in land mass (over 900,000 square miles) and population (estimated 105 million).

ECC—Église du Christ au Congo (Church of Christ in the Congo) is a Protestant denomination that partners with Mennonite Central Committee on the Program for Peace and Reconciliation (PPR) and the Ministry for Refugees and Emergencies (MERU from the French).

EMU—Eastern Mennonite University is a Mennonite liberal arts university in Harrisonburg, Virginia.

EUPOL—European Union Police Mission, which deploys to trouble spots across the world to offer support.

FARDC—Forces armées de la république démocratique du Congo (Armed Forces of the Democratic Republic of the Congo) is the state army of the DRC founded in 1960 as Belgium handed over control of the country.

FDLR—Forces démocratiques de libération du Rwanda (Democratic Forces for the Liberation of Rwanda) is a Rwandan rebel group operating primarily in eastern Democratic Republic of the Congo. Many of its leaders had positions in the Rwandan government or army prior to the 1994 genocide, and some were involved in carrying it out.

Goma—The capital of North Kivu province on the northern shore of Lake Kivu in the Democratic Republic of the Congo. It borders Rwanda, in which the city is known as Gisenyi.

Greg Starr—A US diplomat, at the time of MJ's death serving as assistant secretary of state for diplomatic security, who was appointed to oversee a Board of Inquiry in the deaths of MJ Sharp and Zaida Catalán.

Hausgemeinschaft—An intentional community started by Mennonites in Bammental, Germany, whose residents share cooking and maintenance.

Kamuina Nsapu—A militia in the central part of the Democratic Republic of the Congo that battles the state army FARDC. Most of its rebels are part of the Luba ethnic group.

Kananga—The capital city of Kasai-Central province in the Democratic Republic of the Congo. It has been known in the past as Luluabourg.

Kasai-Central—A province in the central part of the Democratic Republic of the Congo formed in 2015 when Kasai-Occidental was split into Kasai-Central and Kasai-Oriental.

Kivu—The eastern region of the Democratic Republic of the Congo, which includes North Kivu and South Kivu provinces and Lake Kivu.

Lake Kivu—One of the African Great Lakes on the border between Rwanda and the Democratic Republic of the Congo.

Jean-Pierre Mpandi—The leader of the Kamuina Nsapu who was killed on August 12, 2016, by the Congolese state army FARDC, part of the escalating violence in Kasai-Central.

Menno Simons—A former Catholic priest who became a leader of the Anabaptist movement of the early 1500s in Europe. Mennonites bear his name.

Michael Sattler—An early Anabaptist leader who helped develop the Schleitheim Confession and was martyred in 1527.

Military Counseling Network—A program of the German Mennonite Peace Committee formed to counsel soldiers on their rights, military regulations, and procedures, which includes applying for conscientious objection.

MONUSCO—United Nations Organization Stabilization Mission in the DR Congo, better known by its French acronym, MONUSCO, which is the army of the United Nations in the Democratic Republic of the Congo.

Nikki Haley—A former governor of South Carolina who then served as US ambassador to the United Nations in 2017 and 2018.

Robert Petit—A Canadian lawyer appointed to the United Nations to help oversee the ongoing investigation into the deaths of MJ Sharp and Zaida Catalán.

Schleitheim Confession—A document of early Anabaptist principles agreed to by Swiss Anabaptist leaders in 1527.

Sylvestre Mudacumura—Commander of the military wing of Democratic Forces for the Liberation of Rwanda (FDLR) who was part of the Rwandan genocide and wanted as a war criminal. He was killed by government forces in September 2019.

Tshiluba—A language spoken in central DRC. The translation to and from this language was a key aspect of the plot to kill Zaida Catalán and MJ Sharp.

Tshimbulu—A town in Kasai-Central, DRC, near where MJ Sharp and Zaida Catalán were traveling when they went missing and were later discovered dead.

Acknowledgments

WHEN MJ DIED, his family and close friends were asking each other, "Who's going to write the book?"

They trusted me to take on that task and I have had the honor of telling MJ's story.

There are so many people to thank for their cooperation, support and love over four and a half years of reporting and interviewing, writing and editing.

MJ's family and closest friends have been instrumental in crafting a book to tell MJ's story, which in no way ended with his tragic death.

I'm so grateful to John and Michele Sharp for sharing their son's life with me and also their lives. MJ's sisters Erin Sharp and Laura Enzinna Sharp and their spouses Alex and Nick have also been so supportive of this work to put MJ's story into the world while hoping for some privacy themselves.

His best friends Andy Gingerich and Keith Grubaugh have opened their lives to help this story get told. Like the Sharps, they've answered countless questions and offered counsel throughout the entire process. Along the way, the Sharps and Keith and Andy have become partners in this holy work.

Justin Ramer was an early advocate to the family for me to take on the project and has remained a steadfast support as our own friendship has grown. Sharon Heatwole and others also helped advocate.

My lovely and wise spouse/agent/editor Bethany Swope has been an amazing listener and editor throughout all of this and I can't imagine having done it without her. She is my best editor.

Zaida's mother Maria and sister Elizabeth welcomed me in Sweden and were so gracious on the day we spent together in Kalmar and in their home on Öland.

Others who knew MJ, but didn't know this guy who wanted to talk to them, agreed to talk and became part of the collective work of telling this story. They include, but are not limited to, David Stutzman, Robert "Sgt. Bob" Evers, Christoph Vogel, Julie Jolles, Anna Horner, Timo Mueller, Moise Butimbushi, and Emmanuel Billay.

Cathleen Falsani of Sinners & Saints Creative gave input on the book proposal and helped focus the story as it moved toward finding a publisher. Shannan Martin shared from her experience of writing and publishing books and her optimism that this would become a published book.

Early readers of drafts helped shape the writing of the story. Alex Delp, Michael Miller, Jenifer Stuelpe Gibbs and Nessa Stoltzfus all offered helpful feedback.

Readers helping check accuracy included Julie Jolles, David Stutzman, Judy Mullet, Mark Metzler Sawin, John Sharp, Laura Enzinna Sharp, Justin Ramer, and Erin Sharp.

Steve Wiebe Johnson served as a translator for one key interview, not only being a conduit between French and English, but also adding context.

As I traveled, I was received warmly and provided bed and board by a number of folks, including Ken and Leona Gingerich in Albuquerque; Wolfgang and Hiltrude Krauss at Hausgemeinschaft in Bammental, Germany; Miles Reimer and Kathy Landis in Newton, Kansas; and David and Heidi McAlary in Vancouver, British Columbia.

Winston and Sibyl Gerig and Britt Kaufmann and Chad Smoker provided writing cabins on the sides of hills that gave perspective as I wrote.

Over many years, friends such as Chris Serio Martin, Jason Lehman, Andy Wesdorp, Vince Turner, Pete McCown, the late Omar Eby, and the late Marcia Fulmer and others have exhorted me to write a book and shone a light on the path to make it happen. Friends and coworkers from LightBox and the Community Foundation of Elkhart County cheered me on.

People at Assembly Mennonite Church, particularly those in small group Crisálida, have walked alongside during this project and offered emotional support on the hard days.

The boys of ADGC taught me disc golf as I was writing, providing a needed outlet. Flinging hunks of plastic over and over again was therapeutic and the companionship was stellar.

The team at Herald Press always believed in the story and the importance of putting it into the world. Amy Gingerich was invaluable. Laura Leonard, Meghan Florian, Merrill Miller, Joe Hackman, LeAnn Hamby, Joe Questel, Alyssa Bennett Smith, Sherah-Leigh Gerber, Sara Versluis and others on the team took on this project to put MJ's story into the world.

I'm grateful to my mom and dad, Esther and the late Jonas King, who figured out that a wiggly little boy would sit still and listen if they read him stories. So they read me a lot of them and it helped turn me into someone who strings words together as a vocation.

And finally, I would like to thank Michael J. Sharp. I met you several times, MJ, but I did not yet understand the vibrant, remarkable way you lived. Getting to tell your story has been one of the biggest privileges of my life. I now carry your story not just on these pages, but also within me.

Notes

Chapter 2

1 Harry Loewen and Steven Nolt, *Through Fire and Water: An Overview of Mennonite History* (Scottdale, PA: Herald Press, 1996), 83.

2 *Global Anabaptist Mennonite Encyclopedia Online*, s.v. "Manz, Felix," accessed September 12, 2021, https://gameo.org/index .php?title=Manz,_Felix_(ca._1498-1527).

3 J. C. Wenger, "The Schleitheim Confession of Faith," *Mennonite Quarterly Review* 19 (October 1945): 243–53.

4 Norman Maclean, *Young Men and Fire* (Chicago: University of Chicago Press, 1992), 214–15.

5 Larry Nickel, composer, "True Evangelical Faith," Cypress Choral Music, copyright 2013. First performed by Nickel in 1980. Lyrics used with permission.

Chapter 6

1 Tim Kane, "Global U.S. Troop Deployment, 1950–2003," The Heritage Foundation, October 2004, https://www.heritage.org/ defense/report/global-us-troop-deployment-1950-2003.

2 Michael J. Sharp, "Running from the Military Police," *Young Anabaptist Radicals* (blog), September 4, 2006, https://young .anabaptistradicals.org/2006/09/04/running-from-the-military -police/.

Chapter 7

1 Adam Hochschild, *King Leopold's Ghost: A Story of Greed, Terror, and Heroism in Colonial Africa* (New York: Houghton Mifflin, 1998), 38.

2 Hochschild, 67.

3 Hochschild, 84–85.

4 Hochschild, 225.

5 Michael J. Sharp, "On Assignment: Eastern Congo Coordinator," *A Common Place* 18, no. 4 (Fall 2013): 18.

6 Sharp, "On Assignment," 18.

7 Mennonite Central Committee uses project reports to both propose and track efforts. Many of them include the same background information, such as these paragraphs. The primary report where this is found is "MCC-CFGB Project Proposal, Project and Partner Description," April 15, 2013.

8 Michael J. Sharp, "Mwenga Trip Report, 25–28 August, 2014," submitted to Mennonite Central Committee.

9 Greg Warner, "When a Rebel Is Homesick He Might Be Willing to Surrender," NPR's *All Things Considered*, January 2, 2015, https://www.npr.org/transcripts/374574242.

10 Michael J. Sharp, "Walikali Trip Report, 27–31 August 2013," submitted to Mennonite Central Committee.

Chapter 8

1 Joseph Conrad, *Heart of Darkness* (Seattle: AmazonClassics), loc. 5, Kindle.

2 Adam Hochschild, *King Leopold's Ghost: A Story of Greed, Terror, and Heroism in Colonial Africa* (New York: Houghton Mifflin, 1998), 147.

3 John Prendergast and Fidel Bafilemba, *Congo Stories: Battling Five Centuries of Exploitation and Greed* (New York: Hachette, 2018), 20–21.

4 David Van Reybrouck, *Congo: The Epic History of a People* (New York: HarperCollins, 2014), 23; on the enslaved population in the American South, quoting Robert W. Harms, *River of Wealth, River of Sorrow: The Central Zaire Basin in the Era of the Slave*

and Ivory Trade, 1500–1891 (New Haven: Yale University Press, 1981).

5   The timeline here is all from Prendergast and Bafilemba, *Congo Stories*, 20–21.

6   Somini Sengupta, "A Reversal by a Militia of Rwandan Hutus in Democratic Republic of the Congo," *New York Times*, June 28, 2014, https://www.nytimes.com/2014/06/29/world/africa/a -reversal-by-a-militia-of-rwandan-hutus-in-democratic-republic -of-congo.html.

7   Michael J. Sharp, "Fact Checks (all in one email)," email to Greg Warner, September 30, 2014.

8   Michael J. Sharp, "End of Term Report," January 19, 2015.

9   Sharp, "Fact Checks," email to Warner.

10 Charles Kwuelum, "Let Us Not Grow Weary," MCC, May 27, 2021, https://mcc.org/stories/let-us-not-grow-weary.

11 Chris McGreal, "We Have to Kill Tutsis Wherever They Are," *The Guardian*, May 16, 2008, https://www.theguardian.com/ world/2008/may/16/congo.rwanda.

12 "Rwanda: Justice after Genocide—20 Years On," Human Rights Watch, March 28, 2014, https://www.hrw.org/news/2014/03/ 28/rwanda-justice-after-genocide-20-years#.

Chapter 9

1   MONUSCO, "About," UN Missions, last modified April 22, 2016, https://monusco.unmissions.org/en/about.

2   Ibrahim J. Wani, "United Nations Peacekeeping, Human Rights, and the Protection of Civilians," in *The State of Peacebuilding in Africa: Lessons Learned for Policymakers and Practitioners*, ed. Terence McNamee and Monde Muyangwa (Chams, CH: Palgrave Macmillan, 2021), 81–99, https://doi.org/10.1007/ 978-3-030-46636-7_6.

3   Michael J. Sharp, "MCC-DRC White Paper #24: FDLR Narratives," February 2015, 1.

4   Sharp, "MCC-DRC White Paper," 3.

5   Sharp, "MCC-DRC White Paper," 24.

6   United Nations Security Council, "Midterm Report of the Group of Experts on Democratic Republic of the Congo S/2015/797," October 16, 2015, 8.

7   Security Council, "Midterm Report," 21.

8   Michael J. Sharp, "Group of Experts on the DRC extended pursuant to resolution 2198 (2015) End of Assignment Report," 1.

9   Sharp, "End of Assignment Report," 1.

10 Michael J. Sharp, "Group of Experts on the DRC—Resolution 2293 (2016) Individual Research Plan," 1.

11 United Nations Security Council, "Report on the Informal Working Group of the Security Council on General Issues of Sanctions," S/2006/997, December 22, 2006, p. 10.

12 Jason Stearns, *Dancing in the Glory of Monsters: The Collapse of the Congo and the Great War of Africa* (New York: Public Affairs, 2011), 282.

Chapter 10

1   Staffan Lindberg, *Mordet på Zaida Catalán* (*The murder of Zaida Catalán*) (Stockholm: Ordfront, 2019).

2   Lindberg, 52.

3   Amber Peterman, Tia Palermo, and Caryn Bredenkamp, "Estimates and Determinants of Sexual Violence against Women in the Democratic Republic of the Congo," *American Journal of Public Health*, August 30, 2011, https://ajph.aphapublications .org/doi/full/10.2105/AJPH.2010.300070.

4   United Nations Security Council, "Final Report of the Group of Experts Submitted in accordance with Paragraph 5 of Security Council Resolution 2360," rev., August 8, 2017, 33–34, https:// www.undocs.org/S/2017/672/Rev.1.

5   Ruth Maclean, "Congolese Fighters Convicted of Raping Young Girls in Landmark Case," *The Guardian*, December 13, 2017, https://www.theguardian.com/world/2017/dec/13/congolese -fighters-convicted-raping-toddlers-young-girls-landmark-case.

Chapter 11

1 Sonia Rolley, "Chronology: The Kasai Crisis in 30 Dates," Radio France Internationale, August 21, 2017, https://webdoc.rfi.fr/ rdc-kasai-violence-kamwina-nsapu-onu/chronology/index.html.

2 United Nations Human Rights Office of the High Commissioner, "Zeid Calls for Immediate Halt to DRC Killings," February 20, 2017, https://www.ohchr.org/EN/NewsEvents/Pages/ DisplayNews.aspx?NewsID=21205.

3 US State Department, "2017 Country Reports on Human Rights Practices: Democratic Republic of the Congo," last modified December 1, 2020, https://www.state.gov/reports/2017 -country-reports-on-human-rights-practices/democratic-republic -of-the-congo/.

4 US State Department, "2017 Country Reports."

5 Dulcie Leimbach, "How Uruguayan Peacekeepers Found the Two Dead UN Experts in the Congo in 2017," PassBlue, May 29, 2019, https://www.passblue.com/2019/05/29/how -uruguayan-peacekeepers-found-the-two-dead-un-experts-in -congo-in-2017/.

Chapter 13

1 Reuters, "UN 'Utterly Horrified' by Video Appearing to Show Murder of Two Experts in Congo," *The Guardian*, April 24, 2017, https://web.archive.org/web/20170424232037/https:// www.theguardian.com/world/2017/apr/24/un-experts-killed -congo-video-michael-sharp-zaida-catalan.

2 Reuters, "UN 'Utterly Horrified.'"

3 United States Mission to the United Nations, "Statement by Ambassador Haley on the Board of Inquiry Report on the Deaths of Michael Sharp and Zaida Catalan," August 17, 2017, https:// usun.usmission.gov/statement-by-ambassador-haley-on-the -board-of-inquiry-report-on-the-deaths-of-michael-sharp-and -zaida-catalan/.

4 *Deceptive Diplomacy*, directed by Axel Gordh Humlesjö, Ali Fegan, and Ola Christofferson (Stockholm: Sveriges Television, 2019).

5 Nikki R. Haley, *With All Due Respect: Defending America with Grit and Grace* (New York: St. Martin's Press, 2019), 203.

6 "On UN Deaths, Haley Asks Congo's Kabila: What Happened to My List?," Voice of America News, February 12, 2018, https://www.voanews.com/a/un-us-ambassador-responds-to -kabila/4251148.html.

Chapter 14

1 Ola Larsmo and Brian Palmer, *101 historiska hjälta* (Lund, SE: Historiska Media, 2013).

2 Annie Duke, *How to Decide: Simple Tools for Making Better Choices* (New York: Portfolio, 2020).

3 Stephanie Vozza, "What Poker Can Teach Us about How to Make Good Decisions," *Fast Company*, October 14, 2020, https://www.fastcompany.com/90562265/what-poker-can-teach -us-about-how-to-make-good-decisions.

The Author

MARSHALL V. KING is a writer and journalist based in Goshen, Indiana. For more than twenty years he worked at the *Elkhart Truth* as a reporter and eventually managing editor. He has written for a number of other publications and has often focused on food, writing a popular Dining a la King column. He is an adjunct professor of communication at Goshen College and the head storyteller for the Community Foundation of Elkhart County. Born in Arkansas, where his parents met because of Mennonite voluntary service, he grew up in the Conservative Mennonite Conference. He, like MJ, is a graduate of Eastern Mennonite University in Harrisonburg, Virginia. He and his spouse are members of Assembly Mennonite Church in Goshen.